THIN PLACES

Where Faith is Affirmed and Hope Dwells

THIN PLACES

Where Faith is Affirmed and Hope Dwells

by Mary Treacy O'Keefe

Beaver's Pond Press, Inc.
Edina, Minnesota

ISBN 10: 1-59298-112-7
ISBN 13: 978-1-59298-112-0

Library of Congress Catalog Number: 2005904626

Book design and typesetting: Mori Studio
Cover design: Mori Studio

Printed in the United States of America

First Printing: June 2005

07 06 05 04   6 5 4 3 2 1

7104 Ohms Lane, Suite 216
Beaver's Pond Press, Inc. Edina, MN 55439
(952) 829-8818
www.BeaversPondPress.com

To order, visit www.BookHouseFulfillment.com or call
1-800-901-3480. Reseller and special sales discounts available.

For Dennis, Kevin, Sheila, Molly, Maureen,
Emmy, John, Peter, and Paul

In loving memory of our parents,
Bill and Terry Treacy

TOGETHERNESS

Death is nothing at all . . .
I have slipped into the next room.
Whatever we were to each other,
That we still are.

Call me by my familiar name.
Speak to me in the easy way, which you always used.
Laugh as we always laughed
At the little jokes we enjoyed together.
Play, smile, think of me, pray for me.
Let my name be the household word it always was.
Let it be spoken without effort.

Life means all that it ever meant.
It is the same as it ever was;
There is unbroken continuity.
Why should I be out of your mind
Because I am out of your sight?
I am but waiting for you,
For an interval somewhere very near,
Just around the corner.

All is well.
Nothing is past. Nothing is lost.
One brief moment and all will be as it was before . . .
Only better,
Infinitely happier and forever . . .
We will all be one together with Christ.

—OLD IRISH VERSE FROM A CARMELITE MONASTERY, TALLOW, IRELAND

Table of

CONTENTS

PREFACE

I nitially, I wrote this book as a gift to my nine
brothers and sisters in remembrance of our parents, Bill and Terry Treacy, who died in 2002
within three months of one another. The first
chapters recall the end of my father's life and the
weeks our family spent with him during that time—
first in the hospital after he was diagnosed with
lung cancer and later in the hospice home where
he died. The last chapters tell the story of my mother's more sudden final days, in the same hospital
where Dad had stayed. In describing the events of
this sad but sacred time, I started recording the frequent "thin place" moments my siblings and I experienced before and after Dad and Mom died—those
times when we most felt God's comfort and love,
when hope transcended helplessness and signs of
the divine became real.

Later, when I shared my family's story with
friends and acquaintances, they told me of their
experiences with thin places. Some said my family's
story reaffirmed their hope that something wondrous does exist beyond this earthly life. Others
said it helped them recognize their own thin places
and signs, and enhanced their faith in a God who

is involved personally in their lives. And so my book evolved, as books often do, and I began to include the thin-place experiences of others, not just my family's. Because some of these friends and acquaintances became curious about the more practical aspects of my family's story, I also added brief explanations of hospice, centering prayer, mindfulness, and healing touch, all of which were helpful to us and our parents, and someday may be helpful to you and your loved ones.

Ultimately, however, my book focuses on how thin places affirmed the faith of our parents and fostered hope for their children. The source of Mom and Dad's faith was the Roman Catholic religion. Catholicism was the "container" for their spirituality, for the many rites, rituals, and prayers through which they expressed and deepened their personal relationship with God. Were they alive, both would proclaim that their faith had served them well. Their faith resulted in the hope, as promised by scripture, that death would not be the end and that love does last forever.

The container for my spirituality is also Catholicism. But after many conversations with persons of other beliefs, religious or otherwise, my container has become more porous than that of my parents. I am a practicing Catholic, yet my spirituality is not limited to the beliefs of my religion. I love to hear about how God works in the lives of others who maintain beliefs that differ from mine. In this book, however, it is impossible to discuss my parents' faith without emphasizing the Catholic dimension of their lives. In doing so, I don't mean to suggest that thin places are experienced or observed only by those who possess particular religious beliefs. Thin places are moments of grace—gifts freely given to us by a God who loves us all.

Over time, paying attention to my own thin-place experiences and discovering their meaning—in part through my conversations with others I call "soul friends"—has enabled me to see how God truly is involved in my life. I hope this book will encourage you to look for your own thin places. Perhaps like my family, you will be reassured that death is not an end to be feared, but the beginning of a renewed relationship with the God who draws us near here on earth. By noticing and reflecting upon thin-place experiences, you may see, as my family did, that God is constantly communicating with all of us, sending messages of guidance, inspiration, comfort, love, and hope.

Although most of the stories in this book concern my family, others have graciously shared their thin-place moments with me. I am profoundly grateful for the willingness of my siblings and friends to share their stories and for allowing me to include them here. The names and circumstances related to my family's experience are real. With other stories, some names and circumstances have been changed to protect privacy.

Many thanks to my sisters, Sheila Ellsworth, Molly Hottinger, Maureen Lahr, and Emmy Springer, and to my brothers, Dennis, Kevin, John, Peter and Paul Treacy. We shared a very special time during the early months of 2002, and they helped refresh my memory and shared their memories of the time surrounding our parents' deaths. Without their tremendous support and encouragement, this book would not have been written.

Fostering friendships among their children was one of many gifts bestowed by my parents, Bill and Terry Treacy. I feel so blessed to still feel their presence and love in my life.

In addition to my nine siblings, several others read all or parts of the manuscript, including Kay Vandervort, Mary Jeddaloh, Jan Berens, Barb Semerad, Terry Noel, Nancy Sullivan Geng, Janet Hagberg, Alexa Umbreit, Nancy Goldstein, Father John Malone, Pat Walsh, Jeanne Daly McIntee, Jim Healy, Judy Oakes, Ginna Klein, Sue Delaney, Denise Dian, Colleen Corah Hitchcock, Judy Griep, Colleen Szot, Mary Ann Bailey, and Amy Kuebelbeck. Special thanks to my sister-in-law, writer Ann O'Brien Treacy, for her consistent interest and encouragement.

Much-needed editorial assistance was provided by Cindy Rogers, Connie Anderson, Michele Hodgson, and Maria Girsh. Each woman has a special gift with words, and their contributions to the fine-tuning of this manuscript were invaluable.

Milt Adams, Judith Palmeteer and Kellie Hultgren at Beaver's Pond Press were helpful midwives to the birth of *Thin Places*. Thanks also to Jack Caravela, Tom Heller and Jaana Bykonich at Mori Studios for designing this book, including the adept incorporation of my photograph of "the Celtic rainbow," on its cover.

All of us Treacys are so grateful to various members of the Catholic clergy who were incredibly supportive, especially during our parents' hospitalizations all the way through their funerals: Archbishop Harry J. Flynn and Fathers Steve LaCanne, Jim Smith, and John Malone. Additional thanks to Father Malone, our pastor and friend, for his witty and wise counsel concerning both this book and as an adviser to Well Within.

Jan Berens's assistance with our parents' funerals, in addition to her treasured friendship, was, and is, a tremendous gift.

Thank you to our large extended family, including my terrific Treacy and O'Keefe in-laws, to the many friends of my parents and siblings, to the capable staff at Fairview-University Medical Center, and to everyone at Our Lady of Good Counsel Home for all of your care and concern during our parents' final days.

Taking my father's advice to travel to Ireland whenever possible, I wrote approximately half of the first draft of this book during two trips there, in 2002 and 2003. There, I was both inspired and spoiled by the hospitality of Sue Booth-Forbes of Anam Cara Writer's and Artist's Retreat, Father Michael Rodgers in Glendalough, and the monks of Glenstahl and Mount Melleray Abbeys.

I am grateful to Irish theologian and poet John O'Donohue and to Dr. Edward Sellner, for teaching me the significance of "thin places" and soul friendships. I highly recommend their books to anyone seeking a greater understanding of Celtic spirituality.

My profound gratitude and love go to four of my soul friends, who have graciously allowed me to share some of our experiences and conversations, including ones with "Beth" in this book: **B**arb Semerad, **E**llen Glatstein, **T**erry Noel, and **H**olly Cashin. These women and too many other friends to name here constantly remind me of the importance of fostering faith, friendship, family, and fun in my life.

To Colleen Szot, Connie Anderson and the wonderful "Women of Words," thank you for the support and encouragement given so freely each month.

Much appreciation to Jan Bucher for being such a terrific listener and wise spiritual director.

Some of the quotes that begin each chapter come from "Thin Places," a newsletter published by Westminster Presbyterian Church in Minneapolis. Thank you to Pastor Tim Hart-Andersen, the "Thin Places" editors, and contributors Janet O. Hagberg and Reverend John Ackerman for permitting me to use quotes from their work.

Heartfelt thanks to all those associated with the Well Within holistic wellness resource center, including cofounder Pat Walsh, Beth Gedatus, Cindy Lukas, Deb Holdgrafer, and our board, volunteers, supporters, and participants, for all they have done to make my professional life so fulfilling—and fun.

Finally, to the loves of my life—my husband, Dan, and our children, Peter, Bill, Emily, and Tim—thank you for the joy, laughter, and delight you bring into my life.

THE GRACE OF A
HAPPY DEATH

Do not weep over me,
Do not say how sad.
To you my death may seem a setting.
But really it is a dawn.

—RUMI

I first began to understand the phrase "the grace of a happy death" in January 1986. The dying person was my husband's grandfather, Peter Provost, a dear man and the namesake of our oldest son. Several months before he died, Peter and Anna, the love of his life, celebrated their seventieth wedding anniversary. When Dan and I were married in June 1973, Grandpa Peter told his grandson, "Dan, being married to your grandmother has been the most wonderful experience of my entire life." His words gave us the hope that we also might be able to say that after many years of marriage.

Peter was a farmer. He had an eighth-grade education, but he was one of the wisest men I have known. His life was filled with hardship as well as joy. Together, he and Anna survived the Depression, raised six children on a shoestring (including two years when he had a broken back and could not work), and buried an infant daughter. Throughout these difficult times, they maintained an unshakable faith that God would provide whatever they needed, not only to survive but to thrive.

At the time of Peter's death, he was one hundred years old. As the end of his life approached, his daughter Gertrude sat next to him, weeping softly at the realization that her beloved father would soon be gone. Her sorrow perplexed Peter. "Why are you crying?" he asked Gertrude, a sister in the Medical Missionary order who had lived with and lovingly cared for her parents' for a decade. After all, he was about to meet the God he had prayed to his entire life. And he was well prepared to do so.

Soon after Peter asked that question, Anna climbed onto his bed and snuggled close to him, as she had done nearly every night for seventy years. As her husband's breathing became more labored, she knew the end was near. He whispered her name, and in a soft but audible voice he spoke his last words: "Mama, it's so beautiful here." In that ethereal, near-death threshold, when the veil between this world and the next is very thin, his faith was affirmed.

Since then, whenever someone close to me has died, I have thought of that sacred moment and been comforted. That was particularly true sixteen years after Grandpa Peter's death, when my own parents were dying.

Like Grandpa Peter, Dad had prayed all his life for "the grace of a happy death." But I didn't fully understand that phrase until I saw how my father and mother lived out their final days. Dad's willingness to talk about his impending death, and his and Mom's acceptance of the inevitability of their deaths, demonstrated to me and my siblings how God seemed to be preparing each of us for an event that might otherwise be frightening and traumatic.

To be present when someone dies with "the grace of a happy death"—something my parents prayed for as long as I can remember—is to witness the old Celtic concept of a "thin place." The paradox of finding God in the midst of grief became a "thin place" for my family, a time when the devastation of losing our parents was made more bearable by what seemed to be tangible signs that they were happy, at peace, and together again, yet somehow still with us.

As someone who tries every diet known to womankind, I was intrigued the first time I heard the phrase "thin place." I learned about the concept in a book by Edward Sellner, an expert on Celtic spirituality and one of my instructors when I was getting my master's in theology. Having three grandparents who were the children of Irish immigrants, I was curious to learn more about my heritage, especially from a spiritual standpoint. In *Wisdom of the Celtic Saints,* Sellner defines thin places as

> *geographical sites located throughout Ireland and the British Isles where a person experiences only a thin divide between past, present, and future times or places where a person is somehow able, possibly only for a moment, to encounter a more ancient reality within present time; or places where perhaps only in a glance we are somehow transported into the future.*

Thin places are not just geographic, however. A thin place can be an event that results in our feeling a sudden connection to the divine. The experience may result from something we see, as in nature's grandeur, or from something we hear "in the still, small voice" within, as Elijah did when he prayed for death in the wilderness (1 Kings 19:11). It can occur when we have an epiphany—those "aha" moments when we seem to receive wisdom, guidance, or comfort just when we need it most. Thin places may involve other people who seem to appear as human angels, sent to be channels of God's grace and love. Many thin-place times happen just after someone has asked God for a sign and the prayer is answered. A thin place sometimes is accompanied by goosebumps, as though God is tapping our shoulder, sending shivers that say, "Yes! It's me. Pay attention. I am here." One of my friends calls goosebumps "Holy Ghost bumps." Another describes them as "Godbumps."

Marcus Borg further defines thin places in *The Heart of Christianity,* saying:

> *There are minimally two layers or dimensions of reality, the visible world of our ordinary experiences and God, the sacred Spirit.... "Thin Places" are places where these two levels of reality meet or intersect ... where the*

veil momentarily lifts, and we behold God, experience
the one in whom we live, all around us and within us.

In the months before, during, and after the deaths of our parents in 2002, my family experienced several thin-place, goosebumps-producing moments. As we journeyed through the intense grief of our losses, we realized that our thin-place experiences and memories brought each of us much-needed comfort and affirmed our belief in eternal life. We learned that to be present in the sacredness of the dying process can be an amazing thin place.

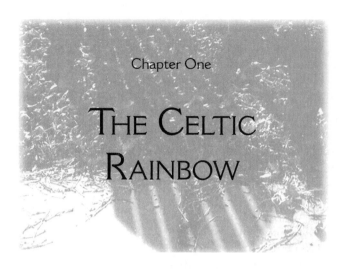

Chapter One

THE CELTIC
RAINBOW

There are only two ways to live life:
One is as though nothing were a miracle.
The other is as though everything were a
miracle.

—ALBERT EINSTEIN

FEBRUARY 5, 2003

I anticipated my friend Beth's call moments before the telephone rang. When caller ID displayed her familiar number, my intuition was confirmed. I had just been thinking about Beth—praying, actually—knowing what she was facing in the days ahead. Her father was dying, just as mine had been, this same time last year.

"Oh, Beth, I was just thinking about you," I said as I picked up the phone. "How are you doing?"

"It's hard—as you know. It won't be long. The doctor said Dad could go at any time, maybe tonight, maybe tomorrow. But because of the Alzheimer's, I almost feel like we lost him long ago."

"I'm so sorry you have to go through this." I hesitated, not entirely sure how she would react to

1

what I was about to say. Yet from our many soul-searching conversations, I knew Beth is deeply spiritual. She, like me, looks for ways God is present in our daily lives. She, like me, often finds the good in even the most difficult situations. So I said what I was thinking. "You know your father will be at peace. And if he goes tomorrow, it would be like a sign, wouldn't it? As sad as his death will be for you, don't you think it would be significant if your father dies on the same day as mine did? Then maybe our fathers will be spiritual friends, just like you and I are now."

"I like that thought." I could hear the smile in her response.

Beth's father did die the following day. The coincidence of losing our fathers on February 6 comforted both of us. Maybe they were together now and would become soul friends, just as their daughters had. Perhaps they were already communicating as Beth and I often did: without words.

Beth (not her real name) is my *anam cara,* a Gaelic term that means "soul friend." One of the many gifts of our soul friendship is that she has helped me become closer to God. In his book of the same name, theologian and poet John O'Donohue describes an *anam cara* as "one of the most beautiful concepts in the Celtic tradition ... a person to whom you could reveal the hidden intimacies of your life." With an *anam cara,* "your friendship cuts across all convention and category. You were joined in an ancient and eternal way with the friend of your soul."

The coincidence of our fathers' deaths became another thing Beth and I have in common. We both come from large Irish-Catholic families, the kind that is so prevalent in our hometown of St. Paul, Minnesota (she has ten siblings, I have nine). We attended the same women's college in St. Paul, although we didn't know each other then. We first became acquainted when we lived in the same St. Paul neighborhood when our children were young. Our friendship flourished after we moved to the same St. Paul suburb, just across the Mississippi River, when we were in our late thirties and our children attended the same parish school.

I remember the day when our relationship evolved into a soul friendship. Several years ago, on the way home from a mother-daughter Girl

Scouts brunch for our girls, Beth and I started talking about our spirituality. By the time we reached her driveway, we couldn't *stop* talking.
Neither of us wanted the conversation to end. It was as if we both
craved this sort of dialogue, where we could freely express our beliefs
without fear of judgment. This was the first of many spiritual conversations Beth and I have had over the years. Becoming soul friends brought
us closer to each other and closer to God. Our soul friendship has
strengthened our ability to discover God's actions in our lives. Many
times, I am convinced Beth is a conduit of God's wisdom, in particular
when she says something especially insightful to me. Sometimes, after
giving me great advice, she will add, "I don't know where that thought
came from. It just popped into my head."

Such heartfelt conversations with Beth eventually helped me figure
out what to do when midlife caused the inner rumblings that so often
precede major life transitions. When I became unhappy—or rather,
unfulfilled—with my long-term marketing position, Beth (a nurse)
encouraged me to become a hospice volunteer. When one of my hospice patients kept telling me I was "like a spiritual director," Beth
urged me to "pay attention to that message," especially after my own
spiritual director (at that time) invited me to join her class on discernment. "Well, *that* was no coincidence," Beth told me at the time. She
believed—and she knew I did—that coincidences are God's way of
leading us while remaining anonymous. Taking her advice, I signed up
for the class and wound up with a master's degree in theology while
also becoming certified as a spiritual director. I began working with
people who live with chronic and life-threatening illnesses, and in
July 2004 opened, with cofounder Pat Walsh, a nonprofit center that
offers workshops, classes, and healing services that help these indi-
viduals cope as fully as possible with their health crises.

In some ways, spiritual directors are like professional soul friends.
A spiritual director listens to others to help them discover how God
is active in their lives, to discern what God is calling them to be and
do. A good spiritual director is not a mutual friend, but a trusted
companion and guide on a person's journey toward spiritual growth.
Tilton Edwards, an author, spiritual director, and founder of the
Shalom Institute in Bethesda, Maryland, explained the spiritual
director relationship when he spoke a few years ago at Westminster
Presbyterian Church in Minneapolis:

Over time, we may find that we are being transformed in ways that enlarge our sense of the divine and our intimate connectedness with all that is. As this deepening conversion evolves, we might experience a certain aloneness that cries out for companionship. This had led me—along with many others—to the particular spiritual practice of meeting monthly with a spiritual companion who is willing to sit with me for an hour and prayerfully listen to my desire for God and the particular ways God's spirit in Christ seems to be moving in my life.

Listening and reacting to what we hear also happens within a soul friendship, but as a two-way conversation in which both persons share their deepest thoughts, feelings, and insights. In my relationship with my spiritual director, I don't giggle or gab about relatively insignificant things as I would with my soul friend.

Beth and a few other special friends had given me emotional and spiritual support during the sad events of the past year. Now she would experience her own loss, grief, and sorrow as her father's life came to an end. My heart ached for what she was going through, and for the grief that still lay ahead.

Thank God she still has her mother, I thought. *I wish I still had mine.*

The past year and a half had been filled with bittersweet memories for me; some brought comfort and others brought tears. The final visits with Dad in the hospital, and later at the hospice, were both touching and sad for our family. After he died, all of us tried to, but really could not, help Mom adjust to living in a house that seemed more than empty without her husband of more than fifty years. Then, before we could recover from Dad's death, we lost Mom. I still cannot believe they're both gone. I still pick up the phone to call them before the futility of the effort dawns on me.

Yet in the months after my parents' deaths, when tears still came uninvited, our family had several experiences that affirmed what we believe: that our parents were happy, at peace, and still with us in spirit. On their birthdays and anniversaries, we saw rainbows and heard their favorite songs. Many such incidents occurred, it seemed, to help us heal. Whenever these signs appeared, we felt connected to the God who, we believed, orchestrated them. I hoped that Beth's family also would experience these signs that brought so much comfort and peace to ours.

A few hours after Beth's call, my family gathered for Mass and a dinner to honor the one-year anniversary of our father's death. During the meal, one of my siblings asked if anyone had noticed anything unusual during the day. Since Beth is also a friend to several of us, we mentioned her father's death. But other than that, nothing out of the ordinary had occurred.

As I lay in bed that night, I mentally visited with Dad, as I often do. This time, I made a request: *Dad, will you ask God to send us a sign to let us know you're still with us? Oh, and please ask for one to be sent to Beth's family, so they will know their father is OK too.* I didn't know whether he could hear my thoughts, but I felt close to him in saying the words.

At 6:40 the following morning, I awoke suddenly—startled, as when you think your alarm clock didn't go off. Instantly, I felt I must go to Mass at the church where we held Dad's funeral Mass. The feeling wasn't a direct command, but I knew what it meant: *Go to 7:00 A.M. Mass today.* Yet I argued with my instinct: *But it's not even Sunday. And it's too cold outside.* A second later, the masculine radio voice that typically wakes me proclaimed a temperature that was harsh even by Minnesota's standards: "It's fifteen below zero today. With the wind chill, it's about twenty-six below. Bundle up, folks." I snuggled even further under the covers. *No way am I going out in this freezing weather.*

But when the intuitive feeling persisted, I knew I had to go. Over the years, I've learned to trust my intuition. So even though I would be late for Mass, I threw on a sweatshirt and a pair of jeans, grabbed a jacket, stuffed my pockets with a pair of gloves, and drove to Assumption Church in downtown St. Paul.

Entering the church as Father John Malone lifted the communion host over his head to consecrate the body and blood of Christ, I hoped he wouldn't see me slip into Mass so late. *Why am I here?* I asked the question like it was a prayer. *Maybe Father Malone will say something especially profound in his homily.* But then I remembered he

5

doesn't give a homily at his weekday Masses. The services ended just minutes after I had arrived. I whined to God as if I were a petulant child: *What was the point of dragging myself down here?*

Driving home, I noticed what seemed to be a vertical rainbow, a single tower of iridescent colors—a phenomenon some call a sundog. I instantly dialed Beth on my cell phone to tell her to look out her window. Beth views rainbows as a sign of the Divine, as I and count-less others do. She and I had heard stories of how rainbows often appear after someone has died. Rainbows validated our belief that nature often is a manifestation of God's gracious design. Maybe seeing the resplendent light would comfort her at this distressing time. I felt certain that this was the sign I had asked for the night before.

When Beth didn't answer, I left a message, hoping she would retrieve it in time to see this beautiful sign of hope. Wanting to cap-ture it in case she missed it, I headed home to get my camera. Driv-ing around my neighborhood, I tried to find just the right vantage point. At a pond near our home, I noticed something unusual about the sundog. Instead of radiating far off in the distance, the filaments of color were shining directly in front of me. Tiny particles of bright light flickered in front of nearby shrubs, not behind them, as you would expect with a rainbow. Later that day, my sister Maureen said she too had noticed this phenomenon.

I took a few photos, then drove to another spot near a small, snow-covered lake and marveled to see yet a second rainbow of the same size and shape, now parallel to the first. Next, at a park where Beth and I often walk, I saw that the two erect beams of light had joined, forming a more familiar rainbow shape. The sun shone brightly in the middle of the half circle created by the arch. I had never seen a rainbow that framed the sun. The radiant light was too much for my camera, which refused to work. Trying for a better angle, I noticed a bird feeder on a pole. Thinking the pole might diffuse the brightness, I positioned myself so the sun was behind the feeder. With one eye squinting through the viewfinder, I was thrilled that the entire rainbow could be seen in the tiny square. In the past, when I had photographed a rainbow, I could never fit the whole scene into the picture.

I dropped off the film for one-hour developing and went home. Beth called, saying she had received my message forty-five minutes after I left it. "I was disappointed because I couldn't see the rainbow out my window, so I assumed I had missed it," she said. "But I was wrong." Minutes after listening to the message, Beth left her home to go to a final meeting at the nursing home where her father had died. Within a mile, she saw the sundog shape I had described. It was in the distance, in the direction of her destination. As she approached the nursing home, the vertical rainbow hovered over the building. The base of it appeared to touch the ground in front of her. The sight of it comforted her, and reassured her that her father was at peace.

"I think I got it in on film," I told Beth. "At least I got a picture of the rainbow I saw. If the photo turns out, I'll bring it to you later." Ordinarily, my photos are never as beautiful as the real-life scene. But this one not only turned out, it proved to be especially poignant. I had captured the entire rainbow, end to end, on the four-by-six-inch photo. Inside the rainbow the sun was not its normal round shape. With the bird feeder in front of it, the diffused light appeared in the shape of a cross. Knowing Beth would love this image, I made a copy for her, and for her mother and siblings.

Later that day, when I brought the photo to her house, Beth found it as comforting as I did. We chatted for a few minutes, then she quickly rose from the sofa and dashed out of the living room, with a quick "I'll be right back." When she returned, she held a Celtic cross, the symbol those of us of Irish descent know so well: a cross whose center is surrounded by a circle. "Look, this photo looks just like the Celtic cross!" Beth said excitedly. "And wouldn't it just be like our two Irish fathers to send us this sort of sign! I'll bet they're both looking down on us right now, smiling."

"I just got goosebumps," I told her.

"So did I!"

We realized that the bird feeder also was significant. Our fathers had loved watching birds at their many backyard feeders. When I told Beth the cardinal was Dad's favorite bird, she said, "My father loved them too. He would often whistle and call to the cardinals and they would sing back to him." (As I write these words on a cold

December day, a male cardinal suddenly lands on the branch of the tree outside my window. There's no feeder on this small bare tree, yet the songbird is in no hurry to leave. He looks at me through the window for several seconds. Maybe it's just a coincidence that my father's favorite bird lingers in front of me as I write about his love of cardinals. Maybe not. But I feel as if God and Dad are here with me at this moment.)

For me, the appearance of the "Celtic rainbow," as my brother Paul has named the photo, was a sign, a thin-place experience, and for several reasons. First, I'm convinced that nature is filled with thin-place phenomena, examples of God's artistry on earth. Second, had I not responded to my intuition and gone to Mass that chilly Friday morning, I never would have seen the rainbow. The experience validated the importance of listening to the voice that speaks within my heart. The event reaffirmed that incredible gifts and spiritual lessons often become apparent when we obey an inner command, especially without understanding its meaning or purpose. Third, seeing the rainbow reminded me how connected we are to family, friends, and even strangers who have died. Just as scripture promises, love is eternal.

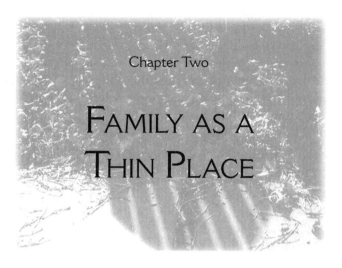

Chapter Two

Family as a Thin Place

In every conceivable manner, the family is the link to our past, bridge to our future.

—Alex Haley

September 2001

Several months before my parents died, Beth and I met for a walk one glorious autumn morning. Our route followed historic, tree-lined Summit Avenue in St. Paul. Various hues of red, gold, and orange were beginning to paint the edges of the oak and maple leaves that danced overhead. The sun picked up the reddish tints in Beth's short hair, and highlighted the faint spray of freckles on her nose.

We hadn't seen each other since the tragic events of 9/11. As we began our three-mile walk, we talked about how the world had changed, how our sense of security would never be the same. We talked about how 9/11 had affected our families. Beth knew that my sisters and I had been planning a trip that month to Lake Tahoe for my youngest sister's fortieth birthday, but that we had canceled

Emmy's celebration because a couple of us were now too nervous to fly. Another sister, Sheila, who lives in Portland, Oregon, was particularly disappointed. She had missed our parents' fiftieth wedding anniversary party, held on September 15, when flights to the Twin Cities and elsewhere were grounded.

"Isn't it a shame we suddenly live in a world where fear seems to dominate our lives?" Beth said, sympathizing with my disappointment over the canceled birthday trip.

"Yes, but I understand why so many people are afraid to fly," I said. "I am too. But it seems more important than ever that we stay connected to those we love. And our little mini-vacations together have allowed the five of us sisters to do that."

We walked in silence for awhile, then Beth asked about the anniversary party. Despite my sister Sheila's absence, and the sad news just that morning that Mom's sister Sheila had died, the party had been a happy tribute to my parents' long and loving marriage. The celebration was meant to acknowledge all they had done for us. Over our parents' fifty years together, we ten siblings had developed a closeness, a friendship that transcended time, space, and a childhood filled with typical bickering and rivalry. There had been tough times over the years, but somehow (with the grace of God, my mother would say), we came through it fairly well. Through the years, I have grown to appreciate how family can be a thin place.

After attending a noon Mass, we gathered at my brother John's home, where he and his wife, Bonnie, served a delicious catered meal. Neither of our parents had been feeling well lately, so we kept the guest list small. The fifty family members present offered congratulatory toasts filled with funny and touching memories. Under a large white canopy in the back yard, two fiddlers played Irish music while everyone danced. We had grown up in a home filled with the music of Irish singers, from Tommy Makem and the Clancy Brothers to Sinead O'Connor (until she tore up that picture of the pope). Dad was delighted with the choice of entertainment, but by the time the music ended, he and Mom were exhausted. As his children and grandchildren frolicked on the grass, our seventy-four-year old father sat on the sidelines. A handsome man in his youth, with dark hair and blue eyes, Dad was big—just over six feet tall and at least 250 pounds. He had always filled the space around him with a vibrant presence. Now, he seemed a bit withdrawn and distracted.

Many months later I wondered if Dad sensed that the September party would be the last anniversary he and Mom would celebrate. Did he know somehow that his life would be over in six months? And that within a few more months, so would Mom's?

OCTOBER 2001

Within weeks of the party, Dad was hospitalized for tests to find out why he had a chronic cough that was getting worse. He had smoked as a younger man, but had given up his Salems in the early sixties. A bronchoscopy revealed "suspicious spots" on his lungs and a pulmonary specialist recommended further testing. At first, Dad agreed, but the day before his appointment, he refused to go back to the hospital until after the holidays. No amount of cajoling could sway him. "Why go back just to hear bad news?" he asked. None of us realized how sick he really was.

Even without an official diagnosis for Dad, our parents had realized some months earlier that their lives would not be the same. In July, Mom learned she had idiopathic pulmonary fibrosis—irreversible scarring of the lungs that prevents oxygen from getting into the bloodstream. The condition is hard to diagnose; there's no known cause. By the time he caught it, her doctor thought maybe she had had it for five years. The only cure for IPF is a lung transplant—not a typical option for a seventy-two-year-old woman.

Our family was shocked. As a golfer and a former high school physical education teacher—not to mention a synchronized swimmer in college—Mom had been physically active all her life. She had never smoked. And she had been in better shape recently than her retired insurance-salesman husband, despite having to wear a back brace to alleviate the pain caused by her osteoporosis. Compression fractures in her vertebrae had caused her to shrink four inches in two years. Dad was devastated when he heard Mom's prognosis. Although he never said it, I suspect he was terrified of living without her. For fifty years, he had benefited from her "put your man first" philosophy that made no secret of her priorities. Mom knew he was

11

worried about her, so she was determined to remain positive. Was she in denial about her precarious health? Maybe. Yet for her it was an effective coping mechanism. She was the queen of positive thinking. One of her mantras was "mind over matter," a phrase that drove me nuts when I was younger and would complain about something legitimate, like the pain of childbirth. I must admit, however, that the wisdom of those three words helped me cope with several problems over the years.

Mom set a goal for herself: to live four more years. Her youngest son, Paul, was attending St. Paul Seminary, with plans to be ordained as a diocesan priest in 2006. She decided she would be there for the celebration. Dad tried to convince Mom that to live that long, she must begin taking an experimental drug that had had some success in treating IPF. My brother Kevin, a physician, emphasized the merits of starting treatment while she still felt reasonably well rather than waiting until more symptoms developed. But she resisted taking the medication when she was told that its side effects—supposedly temporary—would probably cause her to feel nauseated and tired after the first few doses. Perhaps she suspected she would need all her strength to deal with Dad's own uncertain health.

Even before his own lung problems developed, Dad's health had suffered over the past few years. He had been treated for skin cancer and prostate cancer, and he suffered from congestive heart failure. Even so, our parents lived a full life. For years they had toured the United States in a recreational vehicle, with Mom writing missives about life on the road that she photocopied and sent to each of us. They loved traveling, ever since they met as college students working summers at Glacier National Park. They called themselves "penthouse paupers," traveling in style in their cozy RV, yet proud of getting senior citizen discounts everywhere and sharing $1.99 breakfasts at Denny's.

By November, they concluded that their nomadic days were over. The RV would be sold. My sister Molly and I spent an afternoon scrubbing the baby blue and white vehicle inside and out so it would look spiffy to prospective buyers. The next day, Dad left me a humorous phone message, thanking us for our efforts:

Mary, this is your father. Well, the neighbors walking by are still talking about those two gorgeous girls, one on the roof and one with the blasting sprayer that were working here, and they are asking me if they would be available for work on their house. So I've got a few numbers for you to call if you'll be hiring out.... We want to thank you again for the tremendous job you did yesterday. Really great. Bye-bye.

I saved the message, for no particular reason, or so it seemed at the time. A few weeks later, I saved another message from Dad, responding to my invitation to lunch. He had just sold the RV and noted how it was the first time in twenty-six years that our family didn't own some kind of home on wheels. It was a milestone that signaled a new stage of life. I was amazed at how easily our parents understood the necessity of the restrictions suddenly imposed on them. Traveling together had been one of their greatest pleasures, one of many gifts they passed on to their children. Yet their acceptance of their more limited lifestyle and, over time, of the finality of Mom's illness, became a manifestation of the grace they prayed to receive.

Dad's acceptance of his failing health, however, took awhile. Despite repeated reminders and prodding from his wife and children, he refused to go to the doctor and repeat the bronchoscopy. "I'll do it after the holidays," he insisted. Did he know something he wasn't telling us? When I complained to Beth about Dad's stubborn avoidance of the doctor, she encouraged me to back off. "Your father is handling this in the way that seems best for him," she said. "Let him enjoy the holidays. You should too. If there *is* something wrong with him, you'll know soon enough."

Beth's advice reminded me to stop acting like a controlling oldest child. Mom didn't seem to be nagging Dad, and neither should I. Now, with the benefit of hindsight, I realize his decision to postpone a diagnosis was a great gift. Our family would have one final Christmas together with our parents, in blessed ignorance of what was coming.

In the days and weeks ahead, we would know the power of family more than at any other time. We would understand that the love of family, given and received, was a thin place we could retreat to in the coming months. Together in that unique place of belonging, we encountered God's grace, drawing us closer and providing the strength that would enable us to endure our parents' last days.

Chapter Three

LIVING FULLY AS A THIN PLACE

The glory of God is a human,
fully alive.

—St. Ireneas

DECEMBER 2001

Beth and I had always agreed that holiday gatherings with our big families are thin-place times—moments when we feel God's love in the timeless traditions and rituals, when everyone, regardless of age, feels like a child, held with all others in the comfort of God's lap. Christmas has always been the happiest time of year for my family.

Beth knew how worried I was about Dad, but she encouraged me to set aside my concerns and celebrate Christmas joyfully. "Why don't you try to focus on the present instead of worrying about things in the future that are out of your control? That's what your father is trying to do. So should you." She was right, of course. She even chided me to "practice what you preach."

Beth knew that, as a spiritual director, I help people living with serious illnesses to also live in the moment. At the healing center where I work, we teach coping techniques, including the philosophy known as "mindfulness."

MINDFULNESS

Mindfulness, according to Buddhist monk Thich Nhat Hanh, is "keeping one's consciousness alive in the present moment." In *The Miracle of Mindfulness*, author Nhat Hanh says, "Keep your attention focused on the work; be alert and ready to handle ably and intelligently any situation which may arise."

Many people who practice mindfulness find it calms them and helps clarify their thoughts, reduce stress and anxiety, and experience life more fully. In mindfulness meditation, you focus all of your attention on whatever you are experiencing right now. The easiest way to practice it is to focus on your breathing. When your mind gets distracted, just keep coming back to noticing your breathing, observing it but without opinions or judgment. Jon Kabat-Zinn, who has conducted extensive research on the benefits of mindfulness, reminds us, "Wherever you go, there you are."

Dad didn't know about mindfulness—and I doubt he focused on breathing—but he did seem to be trying to stay in the present moment. He was deliberate in enjoying the moments within each day. Over the next few weeks, he would amaze us with his positive energy and clear focus. For now, both he and Mom helped all of us experience the happiness of what was to be our final Christmas together. Mom seemed determined that this holiday would be as carefree as Christmases past.

Our tradition has been that all of the in-state siblings and their families get together on Christmas Eve, then visit our respective in-laws on Christmas Day. We gather at my sister Emmy's house for Christmas Eve dinner; our parents gave up hosting the celebration a few years earlier. This year, as in other recent ones, Dad sat slouched in a comfortable chair all night, letting others bring him a plate overflowing with ham, potatoes, salads, and sweets. Since his bout with prostate cancer, he had gained at least fifty pounds. We gave up trying to persuade him to eat healthy foods. He said he was "winding down" and thus should be able to do whatever he wanted. The Irish fisherman-knit sweater that Mom made him years ago barely fit around his large stomach. Dad didn't care; it was his favorite sweater.

Seated next to him, Mom gently rested her hand on his arm. It was hard to believe she had a terminal illness. She still taught as a long-term substitute at Mahtomedi High School, near their home; we weren't sure her colleagues even knew she was ill. When she talked too much or overexerted herself, she coughed and struggled to catch her breath. This Christmas, she looked older and frail.

Surrounded by happy, squealing grandchildren, our parents seemed content, yet quieter than usual. Dad's belly laugh was not as hearty as it once was. Noticing his lackluster energy, pale color, and uncharacteristic somberness, I had a sick feeling in my stomach. I sensed this would be his last Christmas and, maybe, Mom's too. I took their picture, the last photo taken of them before Dad entered the hospital. The joy and excitement of our Christmas traditions acted as booster shots of energy and love in the weeks that followed.

On December 26, Dad kept his promise and returned to see his doctor. An exam revealed fluid around his lungs, and it was removed at the hospital. He would find out the following week if he needed to repeat the bronchoscopy. A few days later, more grim news: Tumors were found in the fluid outside his lungs. The doctor didn't say the tumors were cancerous, yet he made an appointment for Dad to see an oncologist the following Thursday.

A few days later, realizing he and Mom would now be in and out of hospitals for medical treatments, Dad did something we never thought he could or would: He decided to sell his dog. Mom used to joke that she came third on my father's list of priorities, the first being his mother and the second being whatever dog he owned at the time. Our family was never without a dog, and the long list of pets included dachshunds, basset hounds, lhaso apsos, schnauzers, and, finally, Boots, a Boston terrier. Boots was the same breed with the same name as Dad's dog when he was growing up. Using the Internet, Dad found a good home for Boots with two Boston terrier "rescuers." On December 28, he said good-bye to his beloved pal.

After Boots was gone, we all expected Dad to go into one of his "sinkers," which usually occurred when he suffered some kind of loss. The first sign of these occasional episodes of depression (he was never formally diagnosed) was his flat, negative tone of voice—if he spoke at all. He dealt with sinkers by retreating to his bedroom for a couple of days, only to reemerge and act as if nothing had happened. But if he was depressed after getting rid of Boots, it wasn't obvious to us. Dad seemed as at peace with this major life transition as when he sold the RV. It became apparent that he and Mom were preparing themselves for what lay ahead. Things like RVs and family pets no longer held the importance they once did.

JANUARY 2002

On Thursday, January 3, surrounded by Mom, seven of his ten children, and one sister-in-law, Dad met with an oncologist who specializes in pulmonary cancer. Dad captured this important meeting the way he had nearly every other event in his adult life: on film. Ever since he had bought a videocamera (when they first became available), he recorded everything, significant or otherwise. Why should today be any different? The doctor looked decidedly perplexed when he first walked into the crowded exam room and saw the camera, but he went along with it. After greeting us all, he displayed Dad's CT film on the x-ray box mounted on the wall. He pointed to the shaded areas of Dad's lungs, indicating the ominous presence of tumors. He then delivered the news we all suspected but dreaded: Dad had cancer. The tumors in the fluid around his lungs were inoperable.

As several of us grabbed tissues, the oncologist tried to be compassionate as well as professional. "We can reduce the tumors with chemotherapy, but basically there is no cure." He said he would recommend chemotherapy for two reasons: first, to prolong Dad's life, and second, to relieve discomfort. Hesitating briefly, the doctor then told him about a couple of experimental drugs and other treatments, although he looked uncertain about whether to recommend that

Dad pursue them. He asked about Dad's overall health, especially his heart condition and activity level. Dad's responses were a combination of honesty and denial: "Well, I used to golf frequently, but I haven't felt like playing for the last few months." (Years, actually.) "Oh, and I used to swim at the Y several times a week." (He neglected to mention the life preserver he strapped around his large stomach.) Finally, he admitted the truth: he just didn't seem to have much energy any more.

In response to this confession, the doctor probed further. "Bill, on a one to four scale—one being in decent physical shape, and four being a total couch potato—where would you put yourself?" Dad's answer—"Probably a two"—prompted a few snickers from his kids. The doctor drew his own conclusions: Dad wasn't healthy enough to participate in the experimental drug trials. The options were chemotherapy or nothing.

A surgical procedure was scheduled to remove fluid around his lungs; at the same time a catheter would be inserted in his chest to administer chemotherapy. Removing the fluid was risky, but deemed necessary. Then the doctor said he wanted to examine Dad further, so the rest of us left to wait in a small conference room down the hall. We all wanted to see how Mom, the eternal optimist, was taking this devastating news.

The nine of us fit easily around a large oblong-shaped table, adorned with three phones and several Kleenex boxes. I wondered how many other families had gathered here, reeling from their own bad news. In blessed privacy, we hugged each other and Mom, and reached for more tissues. Mom said she was "fine" and that she and Dad would "deal with this as best we can." As was her nature, she soon became task-oriented and asked if I would call the extended family and friends. She would call Dad's siblings and hers to tell them the news.

"Of course," I replied, "but we'd better get our stories straight. What will you say to everyone?"

"Well," she said hesitantly, "I'll tell them the doctors found abnormal cells in the fluid around his lungs." The spin was beginning.

"No, Mom. The word they used was 'malignant.' We didn't like to hear it, but that's what it was."

19

"Oh, I guess you're right," she admitted.

One of my brothers then asked, "Mom, what did you hear as Dad's prognosis?"

Again, she hesitated, as if saying the truth would make it too real. "He could live up to two years?"

"No, Mom. The statistics aren't quite that favorable. Only 14 percent of the people that get this cancer are alive after one year; 28 percent with treatment. We heard that most of the people live four months, maybe six with treatment."

Were we being cruel in insisting she face the reality of Dad's prognosis? Were we denying her hope? He could fall into the 28 percent group, after all. But this figure didn't take into consideration his overall poor health.

Calling my parents' friends was one of the hardest things I have ever done. Mom and Dad were blessed with good friends who had known them since we were youngsters. Many of these couples had met in a church discussion group decades ago, and they still got together regularly. Mom and Dad each had several other close friends, including people they had known since high school. It broke my heart to tell these special people whom I'd known as long as I could remember that Dad had only a few months to live. The calls were brief. I could barely get out the words before my voice broke.

On Friday, January 4, my brother Dennis took Dad to the doctor for a cardiac check-up. It was good to have Dennis in town; he had driven up from Kansas City with his two oldest sons. Dennis had also attended the consultation with the oncologist the previous day. At the cardiologist's appointment, Dad learned that the fluid around his heart now surrounded his lungs. He was immediately admitted to Fairview-University Medical Center in Minneapolis and told he must remain there throughout the next week, until his surgical procedure could be performed to remove the fluid. As we gathered in the hospital's family lounge, some of my siblings wondered if Dad would ever return home. Others, including me, could not fathom this possibility. The optimists prevailed, and we began making plans to care for him when he did go home, knowing Mom would need lots of help.

The next day, my four children visited Dad. Our oldest sons, Peter and Bill, would soon return to college and they knew it might be the last time they would see their grandfather. They emerged from his room in tears, as did our daughter, Emily. Our youngest, Tim, trying to remain optimistic, told me later, "It seemed like Grandpa wasn't even sick. He was as funny as usual, cracking jokes and asking how we were doing. He even told us he looked forward to sharing a Guinness in heaven with his (deceased) mother." My husband, Dan, and I visited Dad later that evening, since it was hard for him to have too many visitors at one time. His spirits did seem good. If he was depressed, he hid it well.

Dad was living fully, engaged and enjoying every precious moment with his family and friends. For him, living fully had become a thin place. He let his faith calm whatever fears he may have had about dying. He was letting go of the fear of things he could not control, making the most of his final days with a focused, positive attitude. Over the next month, he would join the ranks of people who teach me how to live most fully—those who thrive even while coping with a life-threatening illness.

Chapter Four

SHARING FAITH AS A THIN PLACE

FAITH

Faith is not a destination
Normally achieved in one fell swoop
In a single moment of blazing revelation
But is rather a journey
Traveled in fits and starts
Three steps forward and two steps back

And it is during those times
When our faith is most ferociously tested
That we see the close proximity
Between suffering and faith
Faith and comfort
Comfort and suffering

Therefore think to observe
The comfort in your suffering
For your faith promises you that
At the very least

—MARK PETERS

JANUARY 6, 2002

Beth and I had spoken only sporadically since Dad was diagnosed. She knew I was spending nearly every spare minute at the hospital and she understood. One morning, however, she gently encouraged me to take a break and meet her at Brewberry's, a friendly neighborhood coffee shop. Outside Brewberry's, a sign across the shop's marquee invited interpretation: "Look. The signs are all around." The message, the owner told me, motivated some customers to share their "sign" stories. Inside the building, described as "the best use of a former gas station" by a framed magazine article on the wall, friends leaned toward each other across small square tables in a modern-day version of the coffee klatches of years past. This place always reminds me of the many reasons that I love St. Paul.

Cradling a hot cup of latté—half-skim, half-soy, sugar-free vanilla decaf, to be exact—I told Beth about the past few days, how Mom and Dad seemed to have accepted Dad's prognosis. "But it's hard for me to believe they really feel that way."

When Mom used the word "accepted" with me the previous day, I had said to her, "OK, so you went through the shock. You mean you're just skipping over the denial, bargaining, depression, and anger stages?"

Mom assured me that, although she and Dad had their moments of sadness and grief, they were "dealing with it pretty well." She added: "Actually, we both feel surprisingly peaceful." At the time, I wondered if they were denying the inevitable. Yet Mom did acknowledge there was little hope for either to improve.

When I told Beth that an aura of peacefulness did surround my parents, she nodded. Drawing on her experience as a nurse, she observed, "That can happen with people at the end of their lives, especially when they believe that death really isn't the end."

After we said good-bye, I drove to the hospital via Mississippi River Boulevard. The parklike road that winds along the riverbanks and past palatial homes lends itself to reflection. Long before Mom and Dad became ill, Beth and I had discussed our parents' strong faith, sometimes with envy. I now realized they had prepared their entire lives for the moment of their deaths. Their strong faith reassured them they would soon meet their maker, and be reunited with deceased loved ones.

Observing my parents' reaction to impending death was an inspirational thin-place experience. Soon, Dad's life would end and Mom's life without Dad would begin. She would have to struggle with her own terminal illness without him. They should have been terrified, or so I thought. But Mom's peacefulness and Dad's apparent lack of fear—especially coming from someone who tended toward hypochondria—contradicted their predicament. To me, there seemed no other explanation for their reaction except grace and a God who had given them that grace.

I hoped and prayed with all my heart that they would die peacefully, without pain or suffering. My parents probably also hoped and prayed for this. But I also realized Mom had tried to explain to me that they were at peace with the *concept* of dying, even if it did not come quietly or painlessly. In their own way, which included the beliefs and practices of their religion, they had prepared themselves well. They did not fear death.

I wondered if Mom, who had borne ten children (including twins), ever thought, as I did, whether dying was like childbirth. There might be pain, possibly severe. With her lung disease, it might be terrifying if she found it hard to breathe at the end. But it would be characteristic of her to take comfort that whatever pain or discomfort she felt would be temporary and the reward would be a new life. I believed her when she said that she was ready for whatever lay ahead.

MONDAY, JANUARY 7

The day after my conversation with Beth, I arrived at the hospital at around 7:00 P.M., expecting to see Mom in Dad's room. But she had just left. I was glad to have Dad to myself—a rare opportunity these days for a one-on-one conversation.

When I asked him how he was doing, Dad said the fluid around his heart was not going away and might be increasing. This news troubled him, he said, but he was grateful the problem was identified and he was optimistic it would be solved. He claimed to be comfortable with the medical attention he was getting, and he liked his nurses. "I really like one nurse; he has a couple of children and is very nice. Another nurse doesn't wear a ring; I think she's lonely. She sat on my bed and was telling your mother and me a bit about her life—sounds like it was a rough one."

"You sound just like Gongie," I said, referring to his mother, who always had been so interested in other people.

Gongie (pronounced "Gahn-ghee") had such a sharp wit and spoke so bluntly that our Chicago cousins teasingly had called her—to her face—"the General." She raised five children by herself during the Depression after her husband lost his job and abandoned the family. My grandfather's sudden departure in 1937 forced Gongie to move her family from their large Victorian home in Stillwater, a charming river town east of the Twin Cities, to a three-bedroom apartment on a busy street in St. Paul. She took a job in downtown St. Paul at Frank Murphy's, a women's fine-clothing store, and worked there nearly thirty years. Dad, the second youngest, was ten years old when his father left. Our father had adored his mother.

"You're a lot like her," I added softly.

He took that as a compliment. "Thank you."

"I miss her," I told him.

"So do I," he agreed. "I'm looking forward to seeing her again."

My eyes quickly teared. I didn't want to cry in front of him so I changed the subject. "How are your spirits?" I asked, wondering if reality had hit him yet.

"Well, there isn't much I can do about this, but after all, with my bad heart, I could go anytime. At least this way, I have some time to prepare. I don't like it, but I am accepting of it." He added, "I pray a lot."

"Does it help?"

"Yes, I think it does."

I told him how so many people—not only his friends and relatives, but the friends of his children—were praying for him. He seemed grateful for this. He told me how he and Mom would pray on their knees every night "until my knees gave out." Dad preferred the simplicity of the rosary; Mom was a big fan of novenas, a prayer asking for intercession from a particular saint, repeated over nine days. I told him about the experience of my friend Sheila, whose father-in-law prayed a novena called "The Chaplet of Divine Mercy," which was supposedly given to a holy nun, St. Faustina. Tradition had it that saying these prayers would help produce a peaceful death. When Sheila's father-in-law was admitted to a local Catholic hospice home, the first person he met was a nun named Faustina. Dad liked that. "Maybe I should tell Mom to say that one," he said.

"It wouldn't hurt," I agreed, then told him that my friend's father-in-law died peacefully in the loving care of the Hawthorne Dominican sisters, who run Our Lady of Good Counsel Home in St. Paul. As I did this, I wondered if he was ready to discuss the details of his death. By now, it had become our family's elephant in the kitchen. We all knew Dad's life was ending, but we were afraid that discussing what lay ahead would be too painful, for him and for us. So we danced around the topic, not knowing how to bring it up, or how to make it safe and comfortable for him to talk about, if he wanted to. Dad was an extrovert, like me, and his usual mode for making big decisions was to talk with those he trusted. He once told me that he would discuss such issues not only with my mother, but also with his good friends. "They're like my own board of directors," he said, "and talking with them always helps me decide what to do."

I sensed he wanted to talk about dying—not just about what would happen to him, but also to Mom and to us. I wondered if he wanted to express his wishes, and perhaps talk more specifically about death itself. I decided to share with him an experience I had had years earlier as a hospice volunteer. One of my older patients, whom I'll call Susan, told me that her family was so upset at the thought of losing her that they refused to talk with her about death. So she talked with me. We visited about all sorts of things related to her death: her faith, her speculation about whether there really was a heaven, her readiness for death yet her concern about leaving her family. We began our conversations as strangers sharing stories and our feelings, yet when she died several months later, I felt as if I had lost a good friend.

"As much as I valued our conversations—and I think they helped Susan—it's too bad she was having these meaningful conversations with her hospice volunteer instead of with her family," I said to Dad, watching for his reaction. He seemed to be listening intently, but he didn't say anything. "So, Dad," I continued, "if you can get comfortable with discussing any aspect of dying that you want to share with us, we will get comfortable with it too."

He waited a moment, then replied softly, "Tell me more about hospice care."

So I explained this compassionate option for end-of-life care, when a person with a diagnosis of a terminal illness receives no medical treatment other than the relief of pain and anxiety.

HOSPICE

Some people believe hospice is a place where persons go to die. Residential hospice care centers do exist, but more often hospice is a form of home care for people who are expected to live six months or less. Hospice offers palliative care—the relief of pain, discomfort, anxiety, stress—and helps families to personally care for loved ones at the end of life, allowing many to die in the comfort of their home.

The health care facility associated with a hospice program forms a team of nurses, doctors, social workers, chaplains, and volunteers to help a dying person and his or her family with any physical, emotional, and spiritual needs associated with the process. The team helps foster sensitive, honest communication among everyone involved—patient, relatives, and health-care professionals. A hospice patient might live longer than six months and continue to receive palliative care if his or her condition continues to deteriorate. But other patients might improve enough to be taken off hospice. So there is still room for hope, despite the realistic assessment that the end is likely near.

"It's a shame," I said to Dad, "that more people don't use this valuable service, or that they wait until the last few days of a person's life before signing up for it."

"So why don't more people take advantage of it?" he asked.

"Because accepting hospice care means you must be willing to acknowledge that your illness is most likely terminal. Your doctor must make a determination that you probably have less than six months to live. And you have to be willing not only to accept that diagnosis, but also to share it with your family." It felt strangely clinical discussing hospice care so easily with him, yet he seemed to want to know about it. But after a while, it was time to change the subject. Enough had been said for the moment.

Dad wanted to know how my family was, so I updated him on our activities. He seemed to want to be the father who gave advice again, instead of the patient who was given advice. We visited briefly about what was going on in my life and I asked him for his opinion concerning some decisions I needed to make. After awhile, Dad's thoughts drifted back to talking about faith. He said he had been praying constantly, and mentioned how he enjoyed "meditating."

"What does that mean to you?" I asked, not wanting to assume the word meant the same to him as it meant to me.

For him, he said, meditating was based on the Christian tradition of reading scripture and contemplating certain passages. He learned this method of prayer at a nearby Jesuit center where, for forty-five years, he had spent many annual retreats. For three days, Dad would enjoy a blissfully silent respite from our noisy, often chaotic home. It was a wonderful time for him to reflect on his life, his future, and his relationship with God. Because Dad was so receptive to discussing prayer, I asked if he knew about centering prayer. He said he'd heard of it, but didn't know what it was.

"Remember when Dan and I did Transcendental Meditation back in the early seventies?" I asked.

"Of course. I thought you both had gone off the deep end."

I ignored the teasing and continued. "Meditation is effective for relaxation and healing. It can even lower blood pressure. Centering prayer is a meditative form of prayer, similar to Transcendental Meditation, which is a method of deep relaxation. Christian monks have been doing centering prayer for hundreds of years, and many people find it helps brings them closer to God."

THIN PLACES

In the shadow of death, the walls of the "container" of Dad's spirituality were thinning, just a bit, making him receptive to a new form of contact with God. "Well, at this point, I'm open to anything, so tell me how you do it."

"The process is simple," I said.

CENTERING PRAYER

Centering prayer is a form of silent contemplative prayer that prepares us to receive God's presence and guidance. This type of prayer was popular during the Catholic Church's first sixteen centuries, especially with saints like John of the Cross and Teresa of Avila. Gregory the Great described the Christian contemplative tradition as "resting in God." The tradition was virtually lost after the Reformation. Thanks to the efforts of Trappist monks Thomas Keating, Basil Pennington, William Meninger, and others who seek to follow the words "be still and know I am God" (Psalm 46:10), people of all faith traditions are now becoming closer to God through centering prayer.

To practice centering prayer, select a sacred word and repeat it in your mind while you sit quietly, eyes closed, for twenty minutes. I like to use words that are only one or two syllables long, such as "Peace," "God," or "Jesus." You can also repeat a phrase such as "The Lord is my shepherd." With two-syllable words, breathe in with the first syllable and breathe out with the second. When your mind gets distracted, just gently go back to the word(s). Imagine you are sitting next to God and feeling so close that you don't even need to use many words.

I told Dad how I used centering prayer when I was hospitalized for breast cancer surgery in November 1999. "After Dan and the kids left each evening, I was alone with my fears about cancer and the possibility of it recurring, so I closed my eyes and practiced centering prayer. It calmed me, and I felt like I was no longer alone." He promised to try it. What was interesting was his willingness to experiment with new forms of prayer and spiritual practices that were not rote Catholic. Although meditative prayer has existed within the Catholic Church for centuries, it wasn't taught during our many years of Catholic schooling. With the resurgence of interest in Eastern meditative practices, centering prayer is gaining in popularity with people from a variety of religious backgrounds.

During my visit with Dad that evening, I remembered how I felt when I had faced the possibility of death from my own cancer: the fear, the anxiety, the worry about the future and how my family and I would cope with a life-threatening disease. I wondered how Dad was dealing with these types of feelings. He must have them, I assumed. He seemed to be at peace, but what was it like for him when he was alone, when Mom left him at the end of the day?

When Dad started coughing and found it harder to speak, it was time to end our visit. He offered to walk me to the elevator—a good sign. I assumed he would prefer his own bathrobe to the hospital garb he wore: a turquoise nightgown, tied in the back, covered by a robe that barely fit. "Here, Dad, do you want this one?" I asked, reaching for the robe Mom brought from home.

"Nah, this one reveals a bit of flesh. Let's give those nurses a big thrill as I walk down the hall."

A few minutes later, he shuffled to the elevator, pushing his IV pole, using it to balance himself. He repeated the comment a nurse had made when he complained about having a lot of phlegm and asked her if there was something he could do about it. "Yes," she responded, "Get your ass out of bed and start walking!"

"Did she really say *ass*, Dad?"

He insisted she did, and he loved her brashness. "Besides," he said, "she was right. It really does help if I move around." By the elevator, we hugged and he told me he loved me. Since he had been hospitalized, Dad had said these words more often than I could remember. As each of his kids left his hospital room, we told him we loved him too, knowing all too well that we might not have another chance.

31

I love you, Dad. Why is it necessary for something like a terminal illness to happen before we can freely express our affection for each other? My brothers and sisters and I have always told our children we love them, but not our parents. Perhaps their own reluctance to say "I love you" prevented us from saying we loved them. Mom would write the words in our birthday and Christmas cards, but our parents rarely spoke them to us as we grew up. Mom always told us, "Actions speak louder than words." And by their actions, they left no doubt that they loved each of us deeply. Yet I was so grateful to share these words with my parents before they died.

Later that evening as I lay awake I was thinking about my grandmother, and Dad's comment that he looked forward to seeing her again. It made me wonder if Gongie would greet Dad at the moment of his death. I had been close friends with Gongie (a nickname that stuck when her oldest grandchild couldn't pronounce "Grandma"), despite her living thousands of miles away. She had moved to Los Angeles after retiring to be closer to my Aunt Peggy. Gongie and I often wrote letters to each other, and every year or so, I traveled to her home so we could giggle and gossip in person. She was ninety-six when she died in 1988, yet I never thought of her as old. The special connection I felt to her persisted even after her death. It seemed like she was present in spirit when I had my mastectomy for breast cancer in 1999. Gongie also had a mastectomy, when she was seventy. Knowing that she lived another twenty-six years after her breast cancer diagnosis reassured me throughout my long recuperation.

Once, a few years ago, it felt like Gongie was physically present. It was a year after my breast cancer surgery, and I was attending Mass at the church near the school my children attend. Going to Mass by myself during the week is different than being with my family and hundreds of others on Sunday. This is personal time—just me and a small group of regulars. I consider it time alone with God, yet also a chance to pray with a more intimate group. Most of the regulars know each other, yet they are friendly to me, a stranger who shows up occasionally. During the Mass when the priest requests prayers for petitions, people ask others to pray for friends, family, the world, and their own special intentions. I have asked for their prayers too, and felt the power that comes from such prayer.

That particular November morning, I noticed an elderly woman who looked familiar. She was in her eighties, with white hair and a distinctive nose. I suddenly realized she looked a lot like Gongie, who also had a nose very much like this woman's. Gongie called it her "Roman" nose, which never made sense to my young ears because she was almost entirely Irish. I thought her nose made her look stately and confident, almost regal. When the woman in the church started cooing and smiling at the toddler seated in front of her, I remembered how Gongie had done that with my daughter—her namesake—when Emily was about the same age. My four sisters and I had visited Gongie shortly before she died, bringing our toddlers to see her for the last time. She had greeted her great-grandchildren with the same affection and delight that the old woman in the church now showered upon the little girl.

I had been thinking of my grandmother at Mass just a couple of weeks earlier, when the priest reminded his congregation that November was the month for remembering the souls of those who had died. Worshippers write the names of deceased loved ones in a book placed in the entry of the church. Among the names of others I've lost, I had written Gongie's name: Emily Treacy. Then, at the end of each Mass during November, the lights are dimmed and the priest reads several names from the book as the congregation prays for them. I love this simple ritual.

My affection for Gongie was projected onto the woman in the church. When I offered my hand in the sign of peace during the Mass, she took it, smiled warmly, and said, "God bless you, dear." She had blue eyes like Gongie. When Mass ended and the names of the dead were read aloud, the silent church seemed filled with their love. I felt such incredible love for the dear ones I had lost—my grandparents, my Uncle Steve, several friends—and felt their love for me. I knew they were with God, but also still with me. Tears fell as I saw their faces in my mind. I wondered if this is what is meant by the concept of the mystical body of Christ—united with others, both living and dead, in communion with God. Just as we had been praying that day for all of those who had died, they were praying for us.

Later that afternoon, as I wrote out a check and dated it, I realized for the first time what day it was. It was November 30—Gongie's birthday, and, as it happens, the same day I had had my breast-cancer surgery one year before.

I had never seen the elderly woman before that day, nor have I seen her since. Yet when I am feeling sad about those who have died, I recall the vision of her smiling face and sparkling blue eyes. Like a well-worn favorite sweater, I wrap around me the warmth of the memory of the love I felt in church that day. The experience created a profound thin place for me, an affirmation of the faith my parents had shared with me and my siblings and our children. For a few brief moments, I felt the past, present, and future come together in an unshakable feeling of spiritual connection to all those I have loved and lost. Remembering that moment gave me hope that Dad and Gongie would be reunited after his death. It gave me hope that even after he was gone, I would still feel his love and presence.

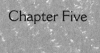

Chapter Five

LETTING GO AS A THIN PLACE

Trust in the Lord with all your heart, and
lean not upon your understanding.
In all thy ways acknowledge Him, and
He will direct your paths.

—PROVERBS 3:5–6

JANUARY 8, 2002

Beth called the morning after my conversation with Dad. I was second-guessing last night's decision to bring up the subject of death with him. "What are you so worried about?" Beth asked. "His doctors have been honest with him. Why shouldn't you discuss it?"

"I'm just concerned that he might become depressed and withdraw from us," I replied. In the past, sometimes a forthright conversation with Dad would seem to go well initially, only to have him stew about parts of it later and have it turn into one of his "sinkers."

"Well, try to let go of your concern. Maybe he was waiting for someone else to bring up the subject. Maybe now he can talk more about his feelings and also let you know what he wants, both now and later. He must have made plans for your mother's care. He was an insurance agent, after all."

As usual, Beth was right. That afternoon, one of my sisters met me in the hall outside Dad's hospital room. "What in the world did you say to him last night?" she asked. Sheepishly, I briefly recounted our conversation, noting I'd promised that we would welcome whatever he wanted to say about what he was facing.

"Was he upset about what I said?" I asked, steeling myself for the worst.

"No! He's suddenly decided to talk about dying. In fact, he won't shut up about it. He's even talking about us getting Mom a new car after he's gone."

Dad had turned his room into Command Central. He was the general, delegating tasks to his minions, just as he had done when we all lived at home. John, a financial executive at an insurance company, and Maureen, who works in the reinsurance industry, were assigned to handle finances. Dad had already done some estate planning to avoid possible conflicts later. Now, he named which of his favorite charities would receive a portion of his modest estate. Molly, an oncology nurse, and Kevin, the eye doctor, became the medical liaisons, in charge of interpreting the news from Dad's various doctors and helping us invoke his living will if it became necessary when death was near.

Emmy, a CPA, would handle insurance details. Peter, an entrepreneur and the techie and video/photography whiz kid (like his father), would document Dad's final days as appropriate, and handle anything computer-generated, like printed programs for the funeral. Videotaping conversations may seem out of place in a hospital room, but Dad, always game, seemed flattered that we wanted to capture his last days on film. My job was to check into hospice options and to be available, with Paul (the seminarian), for "spiritual counseling." Dennis (a surgical supplies distributor) and Sheila (a physical therapist), who came to town whenever they could to help out, would join all of us in our common activity: to pray, both for our parents and for the grace to deal with our uncertain times ahead.

Dad's willingness to talk about his plans for the family and his feelings about dying was a great gift—a thin place that enabled him to remain in his role as husband, father, and provider until the end. And it allowed us spiritually centered conversations that revealed how it was possible to face death, seemingly without debilitating fear. This would be one of his last and best gifts to his family, a demonstration of how the power of faith and prayer can enable a person to truly "let go and let God."

Once he settled the details of fulfilling his final wishes, including Mom's care after he died, Dad could focus on the process of dying itself. His condition deteriorated rapidly, yet he was determined to make his final days good ones. He insisted that he wanted to die with dignity, grace, even humor. And he did. He seemed to realize that these days would provide our last memories of him. He gave us advice he knew we would repeat often when he was gone. One of his favorite lines was, "Keep the faith and the faith will keep you."

Dad never had pain, which was a gift from God. He kept his humor most of the time, but there were occasions when he was less than delightful. No matter how much he insisted that he had accepted his circumstances, he was not exactly the perfect patient. Despite his faith and relative calm, he had moments that left us wondering how he really felt inside. One afternoon, his behavior was reminiscent of his occasional sinkers. When my sister Sheila and I arrived at the hospital together that day, she went ahead to see Dad while I finished a cell phone call to his sister in California. As I was saying good-bye to Aunt Peggy, I saw Sheila hurrying back toward me, brow furrowed.

"We've got a problem," she said.

"What's wrong?"

"Dad is alone in the lobby, and he's *furious*. He made an orderly bring him down there because he refuses to go back into his room. Mom is upstairs trying to learn what happened."

"Why is he so upset?"

"He says he has had it with his roommate."

When I got to the lobby and saw the look on Dad's face, I knew there was no way we were going to get him back into his room. When I asked him what was the matter, he declared, "Either that man goes or I do. And since he's not leaving, I am. He has loud and obnoxious friends who use terrible profanity. Plus, he is watching pornography, with the volume on the TV turned way up."

"Pornography? In a hospital? Are you sure about that, Dad?"

"Well, he watches Jerry Springer. Same thing. You'd think the guy would have a little more respect for someone in my situation."

Worried about our poor mother, left alone to resolve the conflict, I promised to see what we could do and sped off to find her. She was near Dad's hospital room, talking with one of the nurses. I felt sorry for Mom. Ever the peacemaker, she knew better than to argue with Dad when he was in one of his moods. Likely there was no other room available for him, but at least she could try to explain why Dad was so upset. Stressing to the nurse how stubborn he was, I also defended his intolerance of "trash TV." He often repeated to us the words of his mother, who wondered why anyone would "pump dirty canal water through their minds." Disgusted with certain books and television shows, she would say, "Garbage in, garbage out." Gongie had taught her son well: I never saw Dad watch anything that diminished the dignity of another person. He would walk out of a room if a video or TV program showed offensive scenes.

The sympathetic nurse offered to do what she could to change his room, but couldn't make any promises. A few minutes later, one of Molly's closest friends from high school—and, as it turns out, an employee at the hospital—happened to stop by to check on Dad. She offered to check out all the rooms to see if anyone was being discharged soon. Within minutes, she found a vacancy and Dad was moved in. I suspect that his old roommate was glad to be rid of him too. The ten of us and our families probably bugged him as much as his friends annoyed Dad.

Dad's ability to express his thoughts, wishes, and emotions—affection as well as anger—enabled him to say and do things he felt needed to be accomplished before his death. In doing this, he could focus on living as fully as possible in the thin place that resulted from letting go of this life to prepare for the next.

Chapter Six

HEALING TOUCH AS
A THIN PLACE

Our dying has a quality of healing
when all about us are touched by the
recognition of the preciousness of
each moment. Our dying is a healing
when all that has been unsaid is
touched with forgiveness and love,
when all imagined unpaid obligations
of the past are resolved in mercy and
loving kindness.

—STEVEN LEVINE

JANUARY 11, 2002

"Have you used healing touch with your father yet?" Beth asked over our morning lattés, fitting in a quick visit again at Brewberry's.

Beth and I were trained in healing touch, a complementary therapy that can increase energy and reduce stress. "Not yet. I'm not sure he would be open to it. You know how some people resist anything outside of mainstream medical treatment. Besides, he probably would think it's too weird. What do you think?"

"You might as well ask him. It may relax him, and as he gets closer to death, it should help with anxiety."

Healing Touch

Healing touch is a noninvasive technique that uses gentle touch and movement of the hands to clear, energize, and balance the human and environmental energy fields, thus affecting physical, emotional, mental, and spiritual health and healing. Healing touch is one of several techniques that fall under the broad umbrella of complementary therapies known as integrative health care. These therapies complement conventional health care and are used in collaboration with other approaches to health and healing, such as visualization, acupuncture, aromatherapy, and meditation. By using these and many more therapies, along with exercise and good nutrition, people can maintain stronger immune systems, as well as foster their own healing.

In healing touch, the goal is to restore harmony within the human energy system so the body is better able to heal itself. Occasionally, physical improvements, including a reduction in pain and nausea, occur following a healing touch session. More often, according to several studies, healing touch reduces stress and anxiety, thereby helping a person heal spiritually and emotionally, even when there is no physical cure.

I first became aware of the benefits of healing touch when I had my mastectomy in 1999. Reconstruction was done immediately after my right breast was removed, resulting in a complicated surgery that lasted seven hours. My recovery was proceeding nicely until three days later. Coughing frequently, I was diagnosed with pneumonia and pulmonary edema—fluid in the lungs. When my doctor explained the severity of my condition, he warned that I might wind up in intensive care by that evening and could be hospitalized for up to two weeks if they didn't get things under control.

What bothered me most was that the doctor expressed no optimism that I might recover soon. He said nothing that reassured me about my prognosis. I waited for him to say, "The medical team will do everything they can to deal with these complications." Or, "You'll be fine. It will just take time." Instead, his tone of voice and his message alarmed me. I finally asked, "Are you telling me that my life might be in danger?"

"Well, yes. If we don't see a quick improvement, that is a possibility."

His statement sent me into a tailspin. After he left, I felt out of control, almost panicky, as fearful and anxious as I have ever been in my life. Barely able to move, seeing no visitors over three days except my husband, who was with me almost constantly, I was already feeling claustrophobic. The idea of spending another two weeks in the hospital made me feel like jumping out of my skin.

Half an hour later, my friend Mary came to my door but was turned away by a nurse who told her "No visitors." When the nurse told us it was Mary, I nearly shouted to Dan, "Go get her!" and he caught her at the elevator. Mary and I were taking graduate classes together and she had offered to do healing touch after my surgery. I hadn't heard of it before, but said "Sure!"

Mary entered my room carrying a CD player and played *The Pilgrim*, an Irish album that featured "The Deer's Cry." One of our professors had played the song in class and both of us loved it immediately. Mary then asked Dan if he would like to help her. If I would have been more alert, I would have been surprised that he agreed. Even though he had done Transcendental Meditation with me twenty-five years earlier, Dan, like Dad, was skeptical about stuff like healing touch. And I understood their viewpoints. I still cannot logically explain why healing touch so often helps people. But it did help me, almost immediately.

Mary began with a procedure called "magnetic clearing." This technique is used to clear the body of any lingering anesthesia. Mary stood on my left side, Dan on my right. Before she began, Mary was silent, centering herself and (I later learned) asking to be used as a channel for whatever was for my highest good. This is called "setting the intention"; the prayer allows practitioners to detach themselves from worrying about specific outcomes and to trust God. It is important to note that the emphasis is on healing, which can be of the mind and spirit as well as the body. Mary began at my head, then she and Dan gently made sweeping motions above my body, from head to toe, like they were smoothing the area around me.

I don't remember much because I was so tired and weak, but Mary told me later that when they were making the motions above my chest, I started coughing. Afterward, we held hands and said Dan's favorite prayer, "The Lord's Prayer." At the end of the session, I was at peace; the tremendous anxiety I had felt only moments earlier was gone. The words of the medieval English mystic, Julian of Norwich, swirled in my head: "All shall be well, and all shall be well and all manner of things shall be well." My spirit seemed to have healed, and it soon became apparent that my physical condition had improved too. By that evening, my children were able to visit me. By the next day, my lungs were almost clear of the pneumonia. The day after that I went home, even sooner than originally scheduled before I got the infections.

At a checkup a few weeks later, I asked one of my surgeons what he thought about healing touch. "Listen, Mary," he said, "you know you had excellent medical care. But I have seen too much evidence that these complementary therapies help people heal, so I do believe there must be something to them." When a flyer promoting a healing touch training program arrived in our mailbox a few months later, it seemed that this was something I was meant to do.

Dad knew I was trained as a healing-touch practitioner, but he had dismissed it as one of "those things" that existed outside the boundaries of his belief structure. He once referred to healing touch as that "woo-woo stuff you do." (At least he didn't say "voodoo.") Dad didn't understand how it worked, but I assured him it had a scriptural foundation. Healing touch is one way people can "go forth and heal others," as Jesus directed his disciples.

Despite his skepticism, I felt that Dad would appreciate and benefit from healing touch. Unlike some people, he was comfortable with human touch. A great hugger, he had always been physically affectionate with his children. And he loved nothing more than having several small grandchildren sit on his lap. These days he craved Mom's touch, holding her hand constantly. Sometimes they even communicated silently with each other while the rest of us were chatting with them. One time, my mother started giggling, without obvious provocation. When Kevin asked what was so funny, she smiled and said, "Your father is tapping 'I love you' in Morse code in my hand. He learned it in the Navy, and it's our secret code to each other." Our parents were always affectionate toward each other, but during this time they were more open about expressing it in front of us.

Eventually, the time seemed right to ask Dad if he would like me to try healing touch on him. My sister Molly, the oncology nurse, was also there. Before Dad could answer, she told him about a patient she knew who received healing touch shortly before a surgical procedure. During the patient's preoperative checkup, the doctor discovered that whatever needed fixing had been cured. I quickly cautioned Dad and Molly that miraculous cures were rare, but that healing of the spirit often did occur, and this can sometimes also help the body heal. He agreed to give it a try.

After centering myself and praying for his "highest intention," I used the clearing technique that Mary had when I was hospitalized. Dad, Molly, and I chatted throughout the session. When I finished, he said he felt more relaxed and less anxious. Later, he told family members how important it was to touch people, "especially us old folks."

Just as we saw Dad become more receptive toward integrative therapies like healing touch, we would see the benefit of religious rituals. The sacraments of our Catholic religion, including receiving the Eucharist, Penance, and receiving the Anointing of the Sick, were powerful tools for spiritual healing, even though there would be no physical cure for Dad.

On a subsequent visit to the hospital, I was alone with Mom and Dad. I offered to do healing touch again. Dad agreed, adding that he thought it really did relax him. Mom offered to leave, but I said it would be fine if she stayed. "No, you go ahead and have some time alone with your father," she replied. I think she also needed a break from her bedside vigil. After she left, Dad told me how wonderful Mom had been throughout this ordeal. He reaffirmed that he felt stronger in her presence. They were going through this together, knowing they would be losing each other soon.

During this visit, when it was just the two of us, I shed tears in front of Dad for the first time since his hospitalization. He felt sad, but as always he was stoic. (The only time I saw him cry was when my youngest sister, Emmy, was fifteen and hospitalized with a life-threatening infection.) As I did the healing touch, I told him it wasn't just his own children who would miss him but his in-laws too. That morning, as I snuggled in my husband's arms, Dan and I talked about how sad and difficult this time was for both of us. Dan told me how much my father meant to him. Dad had been a special part of his life for nearly thirty-five years, since Dan was fifteen years old. After I told Dad about Dan's comments that morning, he said how grateful he and Mom were for their sons- and daughters-in-law. "Your mother and I always prayed that each of you would find the right person to marry, and it seems as if you all did."

Later, Dad repeated his comment about how important touch was to people, especially to "us old folks." I agreed, saying that even the gentle touch on someone's arm can help lower that person's blood pressure and be healing. We talked about how sad it was that touch could also cause pain when done inappropriately. This conversation took place shortly before news broke of another sex-abuse scandal within the Catholic Church. One of the sad but inevitable ramifications of such scandals is that teachers, clergy, and other professionals must be especially careful with any physical contact, especially with children and young adults

I told Dad about another conversation I'd recently had on the topic of touch. While waiting for my car to be fixed at the dealership, I was seated next to a man who appeared to be in his sixties. Turning the page of the newspaper I was reading, I accidentally bumped the man's elbow. Without thinking, I gently put my hand on his arm, apologizing for disturbing him. He didn't say anything for a moment, then said sincerely, "Thank you."

His reaction confused me. "For what?" I asked.

"For touching my arm like that," he replied. "People are so afraid to touch each other anymore."

The man was a Lutheran minister at an inner-city church, as well as a chaplain at a juvenile detention center. While the kids he worked with seemed hardened on the outside, the minister sensed they often were afraid and confused. Their stories revealed troubled, lonely backgrounds. Sometimes the minister would lay his hand on the young men's shoulders as he spoke with them. "One time," he said, "a tough-looking teenager told me how I was the first man he could remember ever touching him in a nice way. But now I have to be careful. Touching these kids could be misconstrued. It's too bad, because some of these boys have never known anything except violent physical contact."

Telling Dad this story reminded me of another experience I'd had years earlier. On a flight to Minneapolis after visiting my sister Sheila in Portland, I was seated next to an off-duty flight attendant on her way home. The woman and I visited about the seemingly small things people do that can make a big difference in other people's lives. She said her job provided lots of those opportunities. "One day," she explained, "I gently tapped five or six people on the arm as I welcomed them onto the plane. During the flight, each of them told me they were flying either to or from a funeral and thanked me for a gesture that helped comfort them." I asked how she knew which people were receptive to gestures of affection. "Usually, I don't even realize I'm doing it," she said. "But you know, I do wake up each morning and ask God to use me as an instrument of love and grace toward the people I will be seeing that day."

A few weeks later, I remembered this conversation again, at Dad's funeral. As I sat on the end of the pew, friends and extended family members passed me on their way to receive communion, and several people gently touched my arm or shoulder. Each touch created a thin-place moment, when I felt God's love and support motivating the gesture.

TREE LINE

I'm standing, perhaps leaning, at the tree line of my life.
The climb is still uphill;
Yet, my soul is standing on tiptoe
Peering, peeking, trying to contemplate what lies beyond.
Cloud formations might obscure the peaks,
But, the radiant sun beckons from above
And, perhaps, the "thin-place" teases.
Always, I have believed in heaven,
That my spirit lives forever.
But, how my soul continues on is still God's best-kept secret.
Heavenly Father, I thank you for calling me forward ever so gently,
For providing a safe nest for me to rest in when I am weary,
For including Jesus, Mother Mary and my own personal litany of saints
To be present to me in ways of encouragement that amaze me
And, yet, make perfect sense.
Thank you that I have made it this far with a sense of hope,
dignity and trust
And love—always the love.
I know that I can persevere to where I am being called,
That I am being companioned by the very best on these shores
And special guides from beyond.
The possibilities for guidance are awesome and endless.
What a gift to receive them now. . .
And to know that there is life beyond the timber line.

JUDITH F. GRIEP*

---

*Poet Judy Griep was a soul friend who lived life to the fullest during her six-year journey (she refused to call it a "battle") through breast cancer. She wrote this poem after reading the nearly finished manuscript of this book, in October, 2004, and crossed over into eternity less than two months later.

Chapter Seven

DIFFICULT TIMES AS THIN PLACES

JANUARY 18, 2002

Throughout his hospitalization, Dad remained relatively calm. I wondered if his previous run-ins with prostate and skin cancer, as well as chronic heart disease, had helped prepare him for dying. Perhaps it was those diagnoses that allowed him to look death in the face, and to get comfortable with what he saw. Maybe the fear of death that I suspect had plagued him during his episodes of mild hypochondria (he was never officially diagnosed) no longer had a hold on him.

Now that he was near death, I wondered if he was as surprised as we were that he was at peace with his fate. None of us knew what it was really like for him when we left each night and he was alone. All I knew was how I felt at night, lying awake, imagining what life would be like without him and ending up in tears.

Once, I asked Beth how people could seem so calm as death approached. As a nurse, she had observed many people in the final stages of life. "The experience is different for everyone," she said. "Not everyone comes to a place of peace."

47

"Could Dad's previous cancer experiences have helped him cope once the initial shock of his terminal cancer had subsided?" I asked Beth.

She replied, "Cancer can do that sometimes. Not always. Remember how you reacted to your cancer? Not at first, of course, but eventually you accepted your condition. I must admit I was surprised at how calm you were after your surgery."

It's true: I *was* calm after my surgery. But I certainly wasn't calm when I first heard my diagnosis. I suspect that nearly everyone who hears the words "You have cancer" at some point believes it will kill them. I started mentally planning my funeral within days after getting the news. Yet cancer brought me many gifts, including the ability, after a while, to befriend the possibility of death, instead of letting the fear of it consume me. Once I learned how to do this, I was more mindful of living fully, of staying in the present moment rather than worrying about the future. This process was greatly enhanced by the support, love, and prayers I received from family and friends.

This also seemed to be true for Dad. One of the things that helped him most during his final days was the steady stream of friends who stayed in touch. I often wondered what the conversations were like between Dad and his closest friends. He had a great capacity for friendship. Because his three sisters lived hundreds of miles away— as did his brother, Steve, who had died some years before—many of Dad's friends were like family to him. As I have learned more about soul friendships and Celtic spirituality, I have realized that he was lucky to have more than one soul friend himself. (With names like Delaney, Daly, Norton, Gavin, McKinzie, Kelly, and Ryan, his friends of Celtic descent in particular seemed to have some sort of special bond, just as their ancestors may have had with their own *anam cara*.) Most of his friends had known him nearly all his life. I will never forget the heartbreaking moment of watching one of these men leave Dad's hospital room, shuffling down the corridor with his head bowed, wiping a tear from his cheek after they had said their final good-byes.

Nearly every card Dad received told him that people were praying for him. I am convinced that one major reason he (and we) coped so well with his dying was because of those prayers. Before my own cancer, I never knew what it felt like to be the recipient of intercessory prayer, when people pray for another person. To me, being prayed for felt like I was floating atop a cloud that lifted me to a safe and loving place, beyond fear and anxiety. According to Dr. Larry Dossey in *Prayer Is Good Medicine*, a growing body of research supports the healing power of prayer. Physical cures sometimes result and spiritual healing often occurs.

I believe Dad was spiritually healed. Such healing became apparent during another of our conversations when we were alone. We were discussing what he thought would happen after he died. I told him that, based on the experiences of others, I thought I would still be able to talk to him, and possibly hear him if he spoke to me.

"I wonder how that works," Dad said.

"I think it's like a thought—the words come into your head, but you know they're not your own words."

I told him about a friend who heard a voice she thought came from her deceased mother. And I told him about others who asked for help from loved ones who had died, then received what they asked for, feeling somehow that the lost soul had heard the silent request. I reminded him of an event that occurred when his own family was still young.

Before he retired, Dad was an insurance agent. One afternoon, as he was preparing for an account presentation, he became anxious and flustered. This account was a potentially crucial one for his company and his career. He worried that he was going to forget key points of his presentation. "Suddenly," he had told me, "I heard what sounded like several voices in my head. It was as if all of you kids were cheering me on. You were encouraging me, saying, 'You can do it, Dad! We know you can do it!' When I heard those voices, I felt as if I would be able to do a great job with my sales pitch. And I did!"

He smiled at the memory of that incident. "So, maybe that's how you can communicate with us, Dad," I said. "We'll hear your voice as a thought and we'll talk to you in our thoughts—like mental telepathy. Remember how Mom could get you to call her by mentally asking you to, even when she didn't know where you were?"

"I didn't know she did that!"

I realized Mom never told him about that little trick of hers. "If you didn't show up on time for dinner, she sometimes would mentally send you a message telling you to call her. Soon after that, you would call."

In addition to intentionally sending Dad messages, Mom also received them. Once, she interrupted one of my interminable teenage phone calls by telling me I needed to get off the phone immediately. Self-centeredly, I argued with her. "Why should I?"

"Something has happened to your brothers," she insisted. "They may have had a car accident and are trying to call here, so hang up—NOW!" A few moments after I obeyed her, my brothers did call. There *had* been an accident. One had slight injuries, but nothing life-threatening. After that, I had a little more respect for my mother's intuition.

Dad seemed intrigued that this type of telepathic communication might be possible, so I explained my beliefs further. I told him that I believe intuition and mental telepathy are means of divine communication. To me, intuition is God speaking to us in the "still, small voice within," but without using words. This type of communication also reaffirms the spiritual connection that exists between people, not only in this life but beyond it. I am now more attentive to these messages, sometimes even when I don't understand them. Heeding them often leads to a thin-place experience, an intimation of what lies beyond the veil between this world and the next, perhaps where communication exists without words.

After sharing these thoughts with Dad, I teased him: "Just don't talk to me too much when you're gone or I'll think I'm going crazy."

Dad was confident he would be reunited with his family and friends who had gone before him. He repeated what he had said earlier: that he looked forward to "sharing a Guinness" with his mother, brother Steve, and Frank Delaney, his good buddy since high school. "And I am eager to see my father too," he said. This surprising statement revealed at last some healing of a deep wound: that of being abandoned by his father.

My grandfather died in early 1959, nearly six years after I was born. He had managed a candy factory that went bankrupt during the Depression. Ashamed of being unable to support his family (or so we suppose), he told my grandmother he needed to run an errand one morning and never returned. Dad didn't talk to us about his father while we were growing up. I still remember how shocked I was to learn (from my cousins, when I was fifteen) about my grandfather's decision to leave his family, and how angry I was at not having known about it earlier. I confronted Mom, demanding to know why no one ever told us that Dad had grown up without a father. "Your grandmother was a very proud woman, and being deserted by her husband was extremely difficult for the entire family," she explained. Dad had been ashamed of having no father and no money. Instead of going to Little League games and Cub Scout meetings, he went to work, often walking several miles to a factory, where he loaded a wagon with potatoes and sold them on the street.

"But why didn't you tell us about this?" I asked her.

"Because I was told not to. Your father did not want you kids to know, I suspect, because the memories were painful for him. Thank God he had such a strong mother who held her family together despite her own pain." Then she added, "Why do you think your father has been so good to your friends who have had a rough childhood? Because he knows what it feels like to be abandoned, to be poor."

Mom's candid remarks helped me understand Dad and his occasional black moods, especially when he thought someone was criticizing him. I honored her request and didn't mention my grandfather's name to Dad until years later, after I had my own children. I wish now that I had asked him more about his father. With his comments in the hospital, Dad opened the door a bit, but the memory of the admonition not to talk about this family secret kept me from probing any further.

As his life ebbed, it comforted me to know that Dad was looking forward to seeing his parents and other lost loved ones. His ability to forgive his father seemed to create another thin place as he approached death, one where love would transcend pain. Perhaps he hoped the next life would be an opportunity to give and receive love from the human father he never really knew, as well as from the heavenly Father with whom he had such a deep spiritual relationship. I hope, in the final reflective moments of his life, Dad also realized that he had transformed the pain he endured as a fatherless child into a determination to be the best father he could be. He wasn't perfect, but as one of our former neighbors said to me later, "Your father was always there for all of you." And he also was there for our friends.

The difficulties in Dad's life, both past and present, deepened his faith. By his own admission, he was a man of prayer, seeking to enhance his relationship with God. Realizing how much pain Dad had overcome made me aware of how hard times can also be thin-place times, when we receive needed spiritual comfort and healing.

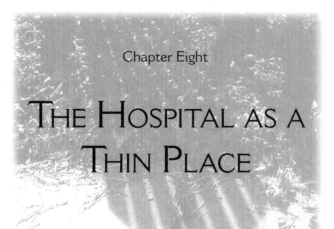

Chapter Eight

THE HOSPITAL AS A THIN PLACE

Let nothing disturb you, nothing cause
you fear, all things pass. God is
unchanging. Patience obtains all; whoever has God needs nothing else, God
alone suffices.

—TERESA OF AVILA

JANUARY 25, 2002

Beth and other friends in medical professions
have told me how the hospitals where they
work often offer them opportunities to witness
deeply sacred moments, thin-place times when they
feel God's presence, especially during the final days
of a patient's life. "Your work is a ministry," I once
said to Beth after she told me how caring for people
who lived in the shadow of death had significantly
enhanced her own spiritual life. She agreed with my
assessment, attributing her compassionate care of
others to her willingness to be a channel of God's
comfort and love during traumatic times.

Thin-place experiences in hospitals often
involve prayer. One nurse I know told me she
often helps create rituals involving prayer and

sometimes music to comfort the families of infants or children who are dying. Sometimes she makes a scrapbook with photographs, clips of hair, or foot- and handprints of the child. She is attentive to the needs of the parents as well as of her patients, and she often becomes close to the families. "I consider my profession to be a calling, something God wants me to do," she said. "Some days are extremely hard on me. And no one told me in nursing school that it would be me, not the doctor, who would turn off life support for a child. But somehow I receive the grace to get through each day."

Substantial research validates the role of prayer in healing. Perhaps this explains why some physicians and nurses now pray with their patients, especially before surgery. One nurse I know has observed several operations when prayer seemed to help during life-threatening crises. Once, when a patient was hemorrhaging internally and the medical team couldn't stop the bleeding, she (and perhaps others in the room) prayed as the doctors tried to save the patient. The bleeding stopped, and the patient survived.

Seemingly miraculous cures do sometimes occur. For our family, prayer would not cure Dad, and after three weeks in the hospital, he ached to go home. The doctors weren't too happy about releasing him, but Dad insisted. He was a big man, and we were all nervous about having to physically care for him. But if he wanted to go home, well, there would be no talking him out of it. Since Mom was getting visibly weaker with her own illness, we all agreed that one of us would have to stay with them at all times once Dad was home again.

On Saturday, January 26, we were told Dad would be discharged the following day. Hospice was put into place; Paul and Bonnie, John's wife, rearranged Mom and Dad's bedroom to make way for oxygen tanks and other necessary medical equipment. That night, the in-town siblings got together at Emmy's house to set up a schedule to care for Dad, including Kevin, who would make the two-hour drive down from Duluth. Each of us would stay with our parents for three eight-hour shifts a week. Calendars in hand, we mapped out a two-week schedule. It took a while to juggle schedules, which left us wondering how smaller families manage to take care of loved ones at times like this. This wasn't the first time we expressed our gratitude that there were so many of us to share the responsibility.

The day after that meeting, we learned that Dad's condition had deteriorated during the night. His doctor told us that Dad's kidneys had stopped functioning. His body was starting to shut down. There would be no homecoming.

January 27 was the last Sunday Dad spent in the hospital. Each of us had enjoyed one-on-one time with him over the past three weeks, but often several of us visited at once. That particular day Mom, Kevin, Maureen, Emmy, John, Paul, and I crowded into his room, sitting on chairs, his bed, and the windowsill. We told funny and poignant stories, alternating between laughing and crying. Kevin thanked Dad for sharing his strong faith with us and, in particular, for recommending that his sons, and later his sons-in-law (including my husband), go on annual spiritual retreats as Dad had done for decades. During one of Kevin's retreats, he was inspired to visit the Caribbean island of St. Vincent and treat poor people who had eye problems. Two or three times a year, he (and sometimes his wife, Ann, and their two children) and a team of medical professionals perform eye exams and surgery for anyone who needs it, free of charge. Kevin credited Dad for the influence these retreats had had on his life.

Kevin also shared his feelings about death, recalling the first time he saw one of his patients die. He said he had not been as sad as he thought he would be, because he knew the man would be well cared for in a better place than here on earth. I was moved by Kevin's story, realizing I had never before seen this side of him. We siblings typically didn't share our spiritual experiences.

The hospital had become a thin place that brought us closer to Dad, to Mom, to each other, and to the God who was caring for us all. The family lounge where we spent hours each day became a sacred gathering space, almost like a church. Together in that simple twelve-by-twelve-foot room, we told stories, broke bread, and shared our fears, hopes, and faith. In the safe and loving presence of family and friends, we experienced God's love.

Despite the sad reason we were together, it was a special time. There were even silly moments that made us laugh. Once, while six of us waited in the lounge during one of Dad's surgical procedures, I got the hiccups and they wouldn't stop. After a few frustrating minutes, I asked if anyone had any good tricks for stopping them. Sheila yanked off my shoe and started whacking the bottom of my right foot. The crowded room was filled with strangers somberly waiting to hear news of their loved ones, but I couldn't help it: I started laughing so hard I could barely get out the words, "*What* are you *doing?*"

"Sarah [her fifteen-year-old daughter] told me this works for hiccups," Sheila replied, and, surprisingly, it did, almost instantly. She later bragged about her efforts when she called Sarah at home in Oregon, saying, "I cured Aunt Mary's hiccups using that trick you told me about."

"You mean you gave her sugar?"

"No, I hit her foot."

"That's not for *hiccups*, Mom. That stops a *bloody nose!*"

The laughter felt good during this serious time in this serious place. The month had passed quickly in the hospital—a grace-filled thin place where we had witnessed our father prepare to leave this life, unafraid and filled with anticipation for what lay ahead, on the other side of the veil.

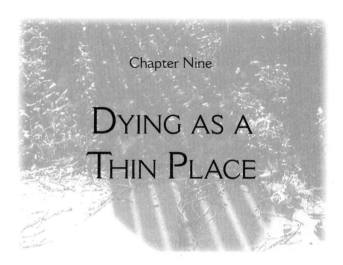

Chapter Nine

DYING AS A THIN PLACE

Nothing can make up for the absence of someone we love.... It is nonsense to say that God fills the gap; God doesn't fill it but on the contrary, God keeps it empty and so helps us keep alive our former communion with each other, even at the cost of pain.... The dearer and richer our memories, the more difficult the separation. But gratitude changes the pangs of memory into a tranquil joy. The beauties of the past are borne, not as a thorn in the flesh, but as a precious gift in themselves.

—DIETRICH BONHOEFFER

JANUARY 28, 2002

As nothing more could be done medically for him, Dad agreed the residential hospice option sounded best. Minnesota has several excellent residential hospices, but our parents hoped Dad would be able to stay at Our Lady of Good Counsel Home in St. Paul. This "jewel of hospitality and love" (according to Twin Cities

Archbishop Harry Flynn) is run by the Hawthorne Dominican sisters. The sisters don't charge their patients' families; they take only small donations from them. (They do accept donations from others, however, and many people designate this place to receive memorial gifts to honor their deceased loved ones.) We were surprised and grateful to learn a room was available on the men's floor of the hospice. Dad was moved there by ambulance Monday, January 28.

Words cannot adequately describe how much the ten days Dad spent in this loving environment contributed to his receiving "the grace of a happy death." The hospice building itself felt like an actual thin place—appropriately so, since the patients here were living in a near-death space. After a volunteer receptionist greeted each of us with compassionate warmth, I lingered in the lobby, embraced by an almost paradoxical sense of being both safe and at peace despite the sad reason I was there. Nuns quietly went about their work, bodies draped in long white habits, faces framed by short black veils. The nearly life-sized stained glass angel that hangs in front of the full-length window overlooking the courtyard seemed a reflection of the human angels who minister to patients at Our Lady of Good Counsel. It felt to me, as it has to others I have talked with, as though the angels and spirits of lost loved ones were present to assist the dying on their final journey.

Within hours of his arrival at the hospice, Dad received a gift for which all of us were grateful: Archbishop Flynn came to give him a blessing. Coincidentally, Paul had run into the archbishop at a recent event. When he learned that Dad was being moved to the hospice, he immediately asked when he could come to visit. The archbishop was one of Dad's first visitors, and he was so excited to see him that he kept calling him "Harry." It was "Harry this" and "Harry that," a burst of familiarity that probably startled the archbishop, who had never met our father. Dad also kept saying, "I'm getting what we all pray for: the grace of a happy death!"

With his characteristic graciousness, the archbishop treated Dad and our family like old friends. Later, however, with a twinkle in his eyes, he did tease Paul as they walked to the parking lot. "Now, Paul," he said, "it's OK for your good and holy father to call me Harry, but that doesn't mean that *you* can."

Archbishop Flynn's visit was a big deal for a staunch Catholic like Dad. For him, life was measured in large part by how he lived his faith, including the rules, prayers, and rituals of the religion he loved. There was a time I was pretty cynical about all this, thinking he and my mother went to daily Mass, said the rosary, and prayed their evening novenas only out of fear or guilt. In my know-it-all teenage years, I often teased my mother about "all this Catholic stuff." I just couldn't accept the idea that if people didn't do just the right things, in just the right way, on just the right days, they might not make it to heaven. I knew enough not to rib Dad, however. You did not mess with his religion, at least "not while you live in this house," as he often reminded us. It was not until after both parents had died that I realized how presumptuous I had been about their beliefs and behaviors.

At the hospice home, our family was showered with thoughtful gestures and kindnesses, occasionally from people we didn't even know. One afternoon, for instance, Peter's wife, Jill, brought friends she occasionally sang with at church to sing a song Dad loved: "Down to the River to Pray" from the movie *O Brother, Where Art Thou?* Music was one of Dad's greatest pleasures. We always had the radio on when we took our many road trips, and one particular tune often became our "trip song." ("The Sound of Silence" was the favorite when we visited relatives in Washington, D.C., in the mid-sixties.) "Down to the River to Pray" became Dad's final "trip song" when he asked the group to sing it at his funeral. It would become a special thin-place experience for our family over the next few months.

Dad's ability to talk freely about his death meant we could ask him about the details of his funeral and burial. He trusted us to decide which readings to use, but he was particular about the music. There were songs he wanted and songs he didn't want. "No 'On Eagles' Wings,'" he insisted, despite Mom's suggestion to include it as one of her favorites. With help from a good friend, Jan, a liturgist, we planned a beautiful funeral Mass that included music and readings that Dad approved. He would be buried at St. Mary's, the Archdiocese cemetery in Minnneapolis. Planning Dad's funeral before he died gave us time to grieve and mourn together in the first days after his death.

When it came to his obituary notice, Dad made a request that seemed out of character for him: he asked if we would get the newspapers to include a feature article about him when his obituary was published. "You know—something like the one when Frank Delaney died," he said. Those of us who were with him glanced quizzically at each other before someone responded, "Sure, Dad, we'll try to arrange that." Later, in the hospice visitors' lounge, we pondered how this promised task might get accomplished. When someone asked, "Who wants to handle this one?" a chorus of voices responded, "Not me!"

What would convince a newspaper editor that Dad was worth a featured obituary? Those articles were for well-known folks in the community, like Frank Delaney. Frank and Dad met in high school and enjoyed a lifelong friendship. Although they had many things in common—both grew up in St. Paul, raised large families, and possessed delightful Irish wits—they were also quite different. Dad made his living as an insurance salesman after serving in the Navy; Frank was a banker, a pillar of St. Paul society who was involved in all sorts of civic activities. Dad used to joke that you couldn't walk one block in downtown St. Paul with Frank without running into someone he knew. Frank's death was newsworthy. But Dad's?

"Well, let's not worry about that particular request right now," someone concluded.

The last days of Dad's life were filled with sorrow, but they were also filled with a grace that manifested itself in tears and—not surprisingly, given his gregarious nature—laughter. One of those special moments occurred the weekend before Dad died. Our mother and all ten siblings were at his bedside. We knew he would not live much longer, so we decided to pray one last rosary together.

When we had finished, Sheila shared her feelings about saying the rosary. More so than any of us, Sheila had a bit of a history of disagreeing with Dad about Catholicism. She's the one who probably strayed most off the proscribed Catholic path, although I admit I traipsed along a few times. Let's put it this way: when our parents visited Sheila, they would go to her church, and then go to a "real" Catholic church because they weren't sure the previous services had "counted." After awhile, they gave up trying to influence her faith and realized that she and her family had found God and a sense of community in churches other than a traditional Catholic one.

So it came as no surprise when Sheila offered this refreshingly blunt comment: "You know, Dad, my family doesn't really know the rosary very well. We like to pray by just talking. That is what I want to do now." She then began what became the perfect group good-bye to Dad. As Mom held his right hand, Sheila held his left. She looked directly at him and told him how much he meant to her, sharing some of her fondest memories and thanking him for being such a wonderful father. She was a tough act to follow, but each of us took our turn while holding his hand. After a few of these sentimental tributes, Paul thought we needed a break. "So," he said, "this might be a good time for a funny story. Anyone have one?"

Molly, a mother of six, quickly said, "I've got one." A few days earlier, she had noticed that her son Kevin, a five-year-old known for his creative use of the English language, had made a mess with his toys, so she asked him to pick them up. In response, Kevin whined, "Mommm—I'm not a pick-up boy, I'm a play boy!" All of us laughed, including Dad.

The "thank you" stories resumed, but when our emotions got the better of us again, Paul asked Molly if she had any more Kevin stories. She hesitated, saying, "I'm not sure I should tell this one." We insisted she go ahead. "Well, last night, I told Kevin that Grandpa was very sick and would be going to heaven soon," she said. "I wasn't sure if he understood what that meant, but his reaction seemed to indicate he did. He said, 'When Grandpa and Grandma go, I'll just call them Die-pa and Die-ma.' Then, grammatical purist that he is, he corrected himself: 'I mean Dead-pa and Dead-ma.'" A few of us cringed, wondering how Dad would react to the punchline, but he let out his trademark belly laugh—the one that makes everyone around him laugh. It was the last one we would hear.

He repeated the words he wanted us to live by: "Keep the faith and the faith will keep you." "Save your money." "Don't touch the principal." Then, he added another suggestion: "Get to Ireland whenever you can." Dad loved being almost 100 percent Irish, and he had traveled to Ireland several times, visiting the small towns where both his and Mom's grandparents had lived before immigrating to America.

Finding the gravestones of family members solidified the connection he felt to the spirits of his ancestors and to the country itself. "There is something special about walking on the land where your ancestors once walked," he explained. Several of us had already visited Ireland and felt that same spiritual connection to ancestral thin places. So promising him we would return was easy.

Later that day, the hospice doctor, a retired physician who worked as a volunteer, told us that Dad did not have much time left and that we should say our final farewells. The doctor explained how hospice recommends four "gifts" or "expressions" that can be shared between dying people and their loved ones. These statements are brief conversation-starters that make sure nothing important is left unsaid, helping to reduce any regrets for not saying such things before a person dies. The four phrases are: "I'm sorry, please forgive me," "I love you," "Thank you," "Good-bye, I'll be OK." Having this conversation often helps both the dying person and his or her family come to a place of acceptance, the final stage of dying, according to Elisabeth Kübler-Ross. In *On Death and Dying*, Kübler-Ross observes, "If members of a family can share these emotions together, they will gradually face the reality of impending separation and come to an acceptance of it together." For our family, her words proved to be true.

In Dad's presence, the doctor recommended that each of us spend a few minutes alone with him and say these words and whatever else we wanted to. "Also," he said, "I want each of you to tell your father what you intend to do with your life and how you will cope with living without him." He encouraged Mom more specifically: "Terry, you need to reassure Bill that you will be able to live without him." Last, the doctor spoke to Dad: "Bill, you must also say these four things to your family and tell them anything else you feel a need to say."

Dad agreed. So far, he had cooperated with whatever the staff recommended, within the confines of his decreasing energy level. But we wondered how many of us would get through this type of conversation with him. He was fading so quickly.

Sheila offered to go first. She spent ten or fifteen minutes with Dad. Peter, Paul's twin, went next. Before he got too far into his comments, Dad cut him off, asking Mom, "Do we really need to do this with everyone?" These conversations were too heavy and exhausting for him now. Besides, each of us had already said as much as was necessary. We had no regrets about what was left unsaid. This was another gift of Dad's terminal illness: the benefit of having the time and opportunity to say good-bye to him. In our own ways, we each had told him "Thank you," "I'm sorry," and "I love you." We were now ready to say "Good-bye."

The afternoon of Sunday, February 3, was unforgettable. Dennis was flying back to Kansas City; Sheila was headed to Portland with two of her three children, who needed to get back to school. Both she and Dennis knew that the next time they came home would be for Dad's funeral. They were the first of our family to endure one of the most difficult moments in life: saying a final good-bye to someone you love. Just before Sheila left, Dad gave her his large, carved-wood rosary. She was so moved that she promised him that she would teach it to her children.

That evening, we each took time to say our last words to Dad. When it was my turn, Dad apologized for not being able to say too much. "That's OK, Dad. How about if I just do healing touch for you?" He said, "I'd like that." So my last conversation with him was mostly unspoken, one of touch rather than talk. I thanked him again for all he had done for me and meant to me, and told him I loved him and would miss him. As we tenderly gave each other a hug, he whispered that he loved me too. Turning to leave, almost without thinking, I asked Dad for a favor. I told him I felt like I should write something, but I wasn't sure what I should write. I had published a few stories, and had started writing a book about coincidences several years earlier, but after five chapters I stopped. Writing is a struggle for me. "So, Dad," I pleaded, "will you try to help me to write from wherever you are?"

"I will," he promised, smiling weakly.

On Monday, February 4, Dad was exhausted but not quite ready to go. I have often heard that dying people sometimes seem to wait to die until someone they wish to see finally arrives. Dad knew his oldest granddaughter, Carolyn, Kevin's oldest, was flying back from the World Junior Biathlon Championship in Italy, where she had just won a silver medal. By midmorning, he asked Mom what time

Carolyn's plane was due in the Twin Cities. "About 2:30 P.M.," she told him.

He sighed and said, "Good."

When she arrived, Carolyn showed Dad and Mom her silver medal. "I won this for you, Grandpa," she told him. He congratulated her and mustered up enough energy for a photo, the last one taken of him. As Carolyn hugged Dad in farewell, he said to her, "It's not good-bye, but adieu. I'll talk to you from the other side."

By Tuesday, Dad was unconscious. And so began the final vigil. He was ready and, as hard as it was to let go, so were we. He had helped prepare us. As if to counter my unresolved doubts and fears about dying, his attitude toward death was inspiring and full of hope.

The in-town siblings decided to stay with Dad as long as we could. The hospice nurses told us he probably would slip away within the next day or two. On Tuesday night, the staff was gracious enough to let seven of us camp out in the visitors lounge. Mom wouldn't leave Dad's side, so we put a mattress on the floor next to his bed. Even from her makeshift bed, she reached up to clasp his hand in hers. My parents did not want to let go of each other, nor would they, until the final moments of Dad's life.

We took turns staying in Dad's room, one hour at a time, while the others tried to sleep in the lounge. On Wednesday, February 6, his breathing was labored and sporadic, but not much changed from the previous evening. Thinking nothing would happen soon, three of my siblings went home to shower and freshen up. At seven-thirty, an elderly nun walked down the hall of Our Lady of Good Counsel Home, ringing a bell to signify that the priest had come to give morning communion.

When someone can't swallow the communion host, the priest or Eucharistic minister will give just a crumb of the crisp wafer. Dad was able to receive that tiny amount. This sacramental act would be the last he shared with Mom after more than fifty years of taking communion together.

After the priest and nun left Dad's room, we were told to wait in the visitors lounge while his nurse gave him a sponge bath. Within minutes, however, the nurse rushed in to the lounge to tell us that

Dad was taking his final breaths. As Mom held his hand and we gathered close around him, the prayers of the rosary were being recited over the intercom as is the custom every morning at the hospice: *"Our Father, who art in heaven, hallowed be thy name.... "* We prayed the words out loud, tears streaming down our faces. People say hearing is the last sense to go before death. I wonder if Dad heard our prayers as he took his last breath. I hope so.

Chapter Ten

RITUAL AS A THIN PLACE

If we stop and let life in our particular community of faith give us new eyes to see, we might catch a glimpse of the Beyond moving close by. Our very people, with whom we worship and work, argue and disagree, pray and hope, love and live, can become a thin place, where God is known first hand. In our thin-place communities called congregations, the veil of mystery surrounding the divine can, indeed, be exceedingly sheer. God is near.

—REVEREND TIM HART-ANDERSEN

FEBRUARY 8, 2002

Beth and I have attended many of the same funerals and wakes over the years, often marveling at how healing these services are for families and friends. But I never fully appreciated the healing power of rituals until Dad died. Religious rites and rituals form thin places, where past, present, and future generations share a common experience of community and worship.

Dad's wake was held two days after his death. In addition to meeting with Father John Malone, our parish priest, and finalizing plans for the funeral, the family combed through our vast collection of photographs of Dad to select the ones we would put on display. This ritual was time-consuming but healing, providing the opportunity to share memories of life with him. All of us inherited his propensity for taking pictures, so there were hundreds of photos to peruse.

Each one captured his personality and love of life: Dad on family trips. Various "Dad and the dog" poses. Dad surrounded by his grandchildren, often with several babies on his large lap. Dad with Mom. Goofy photos too, showing his ability to laugh at himself. One showed him sitting in a bathtub, legs sticking out, knees perpendicular to his large stomach. He was buck-naked, but discreetly so. When I asked Mom for the story behind that photo, she said he once got stuck in the RV tub and thought it was so funny that he insisted Mom grab the camera and capture the moment.

Before Dad's wake, I often wondered how people at funeral homes, including the immediate family, could seem so normal, even laughing during such a somber time. Now I understand. Grief ebbs and flows. Sometimes it begins before a person dies, as it did for us when we were told Dad was terminally ill. His death, even though expected, was one of the saddest days in my life. But there was no time for despair. We had taken care of certain funeral details before he died, but we still had many arrangements to tend to. Planning a funeral is like planning a wedding: similar number of details, but the planning must be done in days instead of months. In the daze of losing Dad, adrenaline allowed us to plan not only the funeral Mass, but also a catered meal for hundreds of people after the service. Or maybe it is grace that gave us the necessary energy.

People told us later that Dad's wake seemed like what an authentic Irish wake must be like: lots of people coming together to pay their respects, sharing stories that bring tears and laughter. Our friends Ellen and Scott, who are Jewish and had not attended many Christian wakes, seemed perplexed by the almost celebratory atmosphere at the O'Halloran and Murphy Funeral Home in St. Paul. "Are you wondering where the tears are?" I asked Ellen, after we hugged and they expressed their sympathy.

"Yes," she admitted.

"The tears have been shed, believe me, and they will continue to be shed," I explained. "But you know what we believe. As painful as it is for us to lose our father, we believe he is with God and yet is also still with us, in spirit. We derive great comfort from that belief. So, with the sadness comes an element of joy, knowing he is happy and at peace. And you are hearing laughter because many of the stories people are sharing about him are funny. Dad was a real character. Besides," I added, "I don't think the reality of losing him has really hit any of us yet, but it will soon."

Ellen is one of my closest friends. After several conversations about the differences in our religions, we have profound respect for each other's spiritual traditions. When our children were young, she invited my family of six to celebrate Hanukkah; her two daughters sang as they lit the menorah and taught my children to play the dreidel game. Her family of four came to our home for dinner during the Christmas holidays, during which we read the Nativity story and sang carols. We both had agreed how we could go almost anywhere in the world and find a church or synagogue where we would immediately feel at home, where the rituals of our religion would be familiar and comforting.

Now Ellen was seeing another ritual that differed from her own, more formal Jewish funeral tradition. I understood her surprise at witnessing the good time people seemed to be having at the mortuary, especially before prayers at the conclusion of the wake turned the mood somber again. But at the funeral the next day, Ellen and Scott saw plenty of tears.

At Dad's wake, another friend shared a poignant story that supported my family's hope and belief that there must be something beyond this life. Mary Pat told us that one of our mutual friends also had just lost her father. I hadn't heard this news and was saddened. I had met the man a few times and knew him to be deeply spiritual. Despite the shock of losing their husband and father so suddenly, the family was comforted by something that occurred just before he died.

The man had suffered a massive heart attack and was rushed to the hospital, where the family learned that he needed immediate bypass surgery to have any hope of survival. He was prepped for surgery. Surrounded by the doctors and nurses who were about to perform the operation, the man suddenly opened his eyes and exclaimed, "I see Jesus." He weakly tried to extend a hand outward, as if to grasp something. As he did, he said, "Jesus, you're here." A few seconds later, he died.

The man's daughter, Pat, told me later that the family learned that every medical professional in the room was affected by this incident. Some were moved to tears; others indicated they were not particularly religious but that the event caused them to reevaluate their lack of faith. When I shared this story with my family, it brought us comfort, just as it had for Pat's family. What a gift to know that Pat's father and family also had received "the grace of a happy death."

And as for the lengthy obituary article Dad had requested, it never did appear in either the St. Paul Pioneer Press or Star Tribune because none of us contacted the newspapers. But to our surprise, Archbishop Flynn wrote about his visit with Dad in an article published in the February 14, 2002, issue of The Catholic Spirit. Beth saw it before I did, and left me a message that ended with, "Well, your father got his wish. Wouldn't he have loved knowing an article was written about him in a Catholic paper, and by an archbishop, no less. I bet this would have pleased him even more than one in the daily papers."

The article discussed the archbishop's visit with Dad in the hospice and how impressed he was with Dad's strong faith. I loved the concluding paragraph, responding to Archbishop Flynn's assessment that "Bill Treacy was well-prepared to meet his God." In it, he imagined what Dad would say "if he could speak to us now":

> *"You may weep if it helps your heart, but if you love me, do not weep for me. If only you knew the gift of God and what heaven is. If only you could hear the angels and saints from where you are and see me among them. If only you could see for one moment the beauty that I see, a beauty that will never fade. Why do you, who saw me and loved me in the land where things pass away, think you will not see me and love me again in*

the land where things never fade? Believe me, when on the day, chosen by God, you reach heaven where I have come before you, then you will see who loved and still loves you. Wipe away your tears and weep—weep no more for me."

I envisioned Dad smiling and nodding his head in agreement to these words—just a little proud that an article indeed had been written about him. I also think he would have appreciated how the rituals of his religion became a thin place for all of us. Through the rites, rituals, and traditions of our faith, we honored his life on earth, as well as expressed our hope that he would be lovingly cared for in the next life.

Chapter Eleven

COINCIDENCES AS THIN PLACES

Mystics are often dragged screaming through the illusions of life, finding greater sanity, serenity and sanctity in the acceptance of God. They were ordinary men and women, extraordinarily alive to the aliveness of God.... God-seers wide-eyed to the color of divinity in every human interaction ... filled with wondrous intuition that every coincidence seeps with the eternal mystery of God and sages of the imagination.

—JOHN POWERS

EARLY MARCH 2002

Friends, including Beth, were wonderfully supportive in the days and weeks following Dad's death. One of the best things they did was simply listen. At first, their compassionate presence helped me process what happened during the time around Dad's death. Later, it helped me cope with the grief of losing him.

In addition to dealing with our own sorrow, my siblings and I focused on helping Mom endure her grief. I never fully appreciated the extent of my mother's love for my father until after he was gone. At his wake, one of Mom's cousins told me that my parents had been a beautiful couple when they were young, so obviously in love. By her words and actions, Mom had always made it clear that Dad's happiness was her top priority.

After he retired, they did nearly everything together, settling into a comfortable life, combining a daily routine with traveling around the country in their RV. Most mornings they went to Mass, then either to the YMCA to exercise or to breakfast if Mom wasn't working as a substitute teacher. At the Y, they would swim together—Mom swam laps and Dad used some sort of flotation device to move around. He would joke about how he spent the morning in the sauna or whirlpool surrounded by "beautiful women." "They can hardly get enough of me," he'd quip, as Mom would roll her eyes.

After Dad was diagnosed with lung cancer, my mother's life as she had known it for half a century was dramatically changed. So many things had been taken away from her within the past year. She had quit teaching, which she loved. The good health she enjoyed for years was gone as her pulmonary fibrosis worsened. And now, Dad's death. "People ask me how I am doing," she told me, "and I don't know what to say. Everything is so different without him. Before, whenever I came home, he always was there to greet me with a big hug and kiss. This house is so empty without him."

Mom's comments reminded me how much she let Dad hold court while she stayed in the background. He loved to visit, while it was hard for my mother to sit because she always had to be doing something. When we offered to help her prepare a meal or assist her, she always said, "No, you just go sit and visit with your father." So we did. I had spent many more hours visiting with Dad, getting to know him better than Mom. Now I hoped I could make up for lost time.

Without my Dad's positive energy, their house did feel vacant; the walls seemed to echo when we visited Mom. After a month or so, she agreed with her children that it was time to move into something smaller. She would have moved years earlier, had the decision been hers alone. My parents certainly did not need a large house anymore, and their two-acre lot, while lovely, required a lot of maintenance. Dad resisted moving, saying, "I'll go out feet first." Now, with Dad gone, she had even less reason to stay. The house was a half-hour away from St. Paul, where most of their children, other relatives, and many friends lived. Plus, she wanted to be closer to Fairview-University Medical Center, where she was receiving her treatments.

With Paul lodged at the St. Paul Seminary, he invited Mom to move into his cozy three-bedroom rambler in Highland Park, a pleasant neighborhood in St. Paul. She decided she would sell her place and move into Paul's in early June. In preparation, we helped her dispose of household clutter.

On my way to Mom's one morning to help her, I stopped by my sister Molly's house, armed with an extra latté, ready for a quick visit. Molly told me about a strange coincidence involving one of our mutual friends, Debbie. Debbie had stopped by to give Molly a laminated copy of the memorial card our brother Peter had made for Dad's funeral. It showed a picture of my father, with his characteristic grin, holding the celebratory cigars that were passed out at his fiftieth wedding anniversary party. On the back was a copy of the prayer Gongie (Emily) had said every day:

EMILY'S PRAYER

God is my help in every need
God does my every hunger feed
God walks beside me, guides my way
Through every moment of the day
I now am wise, I now am true,
Patient, kind, and loving, too.
All things that I am,
Can do, and can be
Through Christ the truth that is in me
God is my help, I can't be sick
God is my strength, confiding quick
God is my all, I know no fear
Since God in Love and Truth are here.

"Where did you find this?" Molly asked Debbie, knowing the laminated cards had been given only to our immediate family as a memento. Debbie told her she was at Sam's Club and found the card on the floor. She had been at the funeral and also knew Dad, so when she saw his image staring up at her, she silently remarked, "Mr. Treacy, what are you doing here?"

Molly and I both laughed as she shared that story with me. If Dad was going to "show up" anywhere after he died, Sam's Club was the perfect spot. Whenever he had spare time, such as when Mom was teaching, he often strolled the aisles at Sam's. He was addicted to shopping there. He loved the store's bargains and the free samples of food.

There could be a logical explanation for the card being found at this particular store. Some of my siblings shop there and so do I, frequently dropping off film for developing at the one-hour photo counter. Any of us could have dropped the card on the floor. But that Debbie happened to find it, at a place Dad loved, and that she knew who it was and where to return it—well, all of that seemed a bit too serendipitous. But God seems to work through events that have logical explanations too, not just through miraculous or inexplicable events. I wondered if both God and Dad were reminding me to pay attention, as Beth so often did.

The coincidental appearance of the memorial card was followed by another significant discovery a few hours later as Mom and I began cleaning out Dad's former study. Most of the memorabilia accumulated over their marriage was crammed into file cabinets and stuffed into bags in this small room overlooking their front yard. This became one of my favorite tasks: sitting with Mom to "go through the stuff." It gave us time for the conversations I craved with her. She actually sat still, sometimes for a couple of hours at a time, as we examined every scrap and file, deciding whether to save or toss it. What a pack rat Dad was! The cabinets and bags contained old receipts, ancient financial records, and copious notes that he made regarding subjects such as how to play golf.

As we sorted through the paper remnants of their years together, I found a tattered shoebox at the bottom of a paper bag. The box held a treasure-trove of memorabilia that Gongie had saved over the years and that Dad's brother-in-law, John, had sent to my parents after she died: Christmas cards from Dan and me, including photos of our children when they were younger. Notes and pictures from my siblings. Birthday and Mother's Day cards for grandmothers. Beneath the cards and photos was a plastic bag filled with faded letters, appearing to be much older than ours. My mother said she had never seen the bag before. I recognized the familiar scrawl of Dad's handwriting on the envelopes, addressed to his mother. Most were dated from May to August 1945. He had entered the Navy that spring, two months before he was scheduled to graduate from high school. Reading portions of his letters to his mother and siblings was fascinating for Mom and me. They vividly described his career as a Navy man, which ended almost as soon as it began: World War II had ended in Europe by the time he shipped out to the Pacific; soon after Japan surrendered, he (and countless other GIs) was discharged.

At the bottom of Gongie's box lay a bulky envelope, postmarked February 1959. Inside was a twelve-page letter from Dad to his mother, written after he traveled to Alaska to bury his father.

My grandfather briefly came back into the lives of his wife, who never divorced him, and his children, who were adults with families of their own. In the summer of 1958, we lived in Phoenix, Arizona, where Dad sold insurance. We drove to Los Angeles to visit Gongie and my grandfather, who had returned to see his family after an absence of more than twenty years. I had forgotten this event because I was just six at the time. But I was reminded of it some twenty years later, during a conversation with my grandmother. Unlike Dad, she did speak a little about what happened when my grandfather left his family. Apparently, there had been some contact between the two of them over the years. Despite his absence, he had kept abreast of what happened to his family. Eventually, he moved to Fairbanks, Alaska.

On one of my frequent visits to see Gongie, she told me that when my grandfather came to visit her in California in 1958, he had sought reconciliation with her and their children. "I actually considered getting back together with him," she said. She even went to Alaska "to see if it would work." But after her visit, she realized she could never live with her estranged husband again. A few months later, my grand-father died.

My mother said he died of a broken heart. I knew from Mom that Dad went to Alaska to bury his father. Just a few years ago, my parents traveled to Alaska to place a marker on my grandfather's grave. Mom told us that this experience was deeply healing for Dad.

I imagined my grandfather must have been terribly lonely through-out his life. Finding the letter Dad wrote corrected some of my assumptions. It also shed a glimmer of light on the man who was his father. In the letter, Dad first wrote about the flight to Fairbanks; he was comforted by a priest who happened to sit next to him. He described the priest as being "as fine a man as I've ever met and his observations and thoughts would console and put the tragic mission I seemed to be on in perfect perspective." Upon his arrival, Dad was met by another priest, Father B., who knew my grandfather well. Apparently, he went to daily Mass and was well liked by many people. Dad wrote, "Father B. stressed in his beautiful remarks at church the keen insight all the clergy and nuns had toward him, his weaknesses, and perseverance to overcome them. Father stated he had never known anyone as diligent and frequent in the practice of his faith, and, as he said, 'be it –50 degrees he would be at Mass and communion every day.'"

Also meeting Dad at the airport was a friendly couple who "were wonderful people, knew Dad equally as well as his other fine friends, whose home was where I stayed. Fairbanks is a town of many nice people and he knew practically everyone there."

Dad visited with several other folks who had worked with his father. They helped Dad learn about the father he never really knew. His friends knew our grandfather had left his family, yet they told Dad that his father often spoke of his children with affection and pride. Hearing these words must have meant a great deal to Dad, who must have grown up wondering if his father ever thought of him at all. Dad also talked to other co-workers and friends, who told him many positive things about his father. Dad ended his letter with a paragraph that indicated how healing the trip had been for him:

I talked to many people these last 36 hours and I can only summarize a few thoughts: I feel a tremendous appreciation and satisfaction having made this trip. I found a great respect for him by people up here . . . the only true way to find the "why" of life is to pray and await the place where he is now, I'm sure; and he is no longer puzzled with the unhappiness and "whys" life sometimes brings to all of us.

After burying his father, Dad flew back and, coincidentally, was seated next to the same priest who flew to Alaska with him. The priest told Dad he had said a special Mass in memory of his father. The two priests and kind people of Fairbanks all came into Dad's life, it seems to me, to help him cope with the most difficult task he ever had to do.

Finding this letter was significant for several reasons. First, it revealed something not only about my grandfather, but also about what the experience of burying him had been like for Dad. The letter demonstrated that no matter how troubled my grandfather had been, he had made a life for himself. It was not the life he could have had, but despite whatever pain and shame caused him to abandon his family, he survived. He was a flawed man but also a good man. He had been liked by all who knew him. Dad's letter to his mother was gentle and reassuring. He expressed no anger or bitterness. Reading between the lines, it's apparent he was grateful for what he learned and experienced on that difficult journey. As a devout Catholic, Dad must have been consoled to learn that his father also had a strong faith. I too find comfort knowing that faith helped my grandfather deal with the regrets he must have had about his life.

The second reason this letter was significant was because it seemed as if Dad had wanted us to find it. It was not the only letter he had written concerning his father. After Dad's funeral, Mom read us another letter, this one penned in the mid-1980s, then stored in a safe deposit box to be opened after his death. In that letter, Dad told us what he knew about his father and conveyed his feelings toward the man. He was saddened to have grown up without his father's presence in his life, but nothing he wrote suggested any anger or bitterness at being abandoned. The letter found at Mom's house was written as Dad was actually living the experience of burying his father, and thus provided specific details about that event. Perhaps Dad wanted us to know more about the man he never spoke of. Perhaps that's why we found the prayer card from Dad's funeral just before finding the letter. I like to think of the two of them now reunited, along with Gongie and Uncle Steve. Perhaps, with the barriers that once hindered their relationship now gone, they are a family again.

Third, this letter demonstrated yet another example of a thin place, when it was possible to find grace in the midst of grief. Certainly, the circumstances of my grandfather's death were far different from those of my father. There was no loving family present, no final words of bedside advice. Yet even in the painful, tragic circumstance of his father's life and death, Dad had received the grace that helped him complete this heartbreaking task. The two priests had been the perfect instruments of God's love and consolation. The friends and co-workers of my grandfather had been that as well. All those people showed up in Dad's life, at that time, for a reason. Through them, he experienced God's grace. I think Dad wanted us to know that.

Last, that we even found this letter at all was a small miracle. It was yet another important item that survived a fire that had destroyed my parents' home several years earlier. And there were several coincidences that surrounded that event, reminding our family that God was indeed present during that stressful time.

The house my parents built in 1973 was further evidence of their ability to live well on a modest income. One of Dad's friends developed Dellwood Hills Golf Course, not far from where we grew up in White Bear Lake. When the friend offered to sell Dad, an avid golfer, a prime two-acre lot on the course, Dad leaped at the opportunity. The lot was priced fairly, but my parents could not afford to spend much on the house itself. Consistent with their "penthouse pauper" lifestyle, they purchased a low-cost, prefabricated model that was built at a factory, then assembled in days on the lot. The house was large, with five bedrooms and plenty of room for a family of the remaining nine kids, since I was married two weeks before they moved in.

Late on the afternoon of July 18, 1989, I received a frantic call from one of my sisters: "Mom and Dad's house burned down!" Fortunately, no one was home; Mom was at her sister's cabin and Dad was running errands (probably at Sam's Club). This meant, however, that no one was able to retrieve irreplaceable family mementos. During the twenty-mile drive to my parents' home, tears rolled down my cheeks as I thought about the destruction of so many keepsakes of my youth. Then I heard a voice in my head: *It's only stuff, you know.* The words were not spoken out loud, but the message was clear, distinct, and comforting.

When my mother arrived, we surrounded her and gently led her to the charred remains of her home. Though she knew she was returning to a disaster, seeing the remains of her home was still a shock. Fortunately, the firefighters had arrived within minutes of receiving a call from golfing friends who saw the fire. The firefighters were able to save the room containing many of our photo albums. When my mother saw the albums, she told us she was grateful that a few weeks earlier she had followed an inexplicable urge (her intuition, again) to move them from one room, now destroyed, into the only room left untouched by the blaze: their study, which was filled with scrapbooks and photos.

But we had lost many sentimental things, including hundreds of home movies, woodcarvings made by our mother's father, and our Christmas decorations. My mother had saved the homemade ornaments her children had made throughout grade school, and I had loved showing them to my own children each year. Among the most treasured holiday possessions were ten Christmas stockings, one for each of us, handmade by our now-deceased maternal grandmother. A Christmas stocking was one of the first gifts Gram would give her newest grandchild. Because I was one of the oldest, I had often stood next to her, mesmerized, as she carefully stitched each new stocking by hand. She decorated them with felt shapes of trains, angels, and (my favorite) Christmas trees, covered with brightly colored ornaments.

My brother John was convinced, against all reason, that these special remembrances of Gram had survived the blaze. He searched through mound after mound of ashes and unrecognizable blobs of burned remains. Finally, he found the stockings, in a box under what remained of the basement stairwell. Also in the box was another remarkably unscathed treasure: our nativity set.

None of this, however, was a match for what occurred a couple of months later on September 15, my parents' wedding anniversary. After church, Mom and Dad drove to the site for a last look at the remains of their home. By now, it had been bulldozed, and a crew was coming soon to clear away the last traces of the building so that they could rebuild. As my parents approached the site, which was still wet from a heavy rain the night before, they spotted something white on the sidewalk. My mother gasped as she bent to pick up the object. It was the prayer book she had carried down the aisle thirty-eight years ago, to the day. And it was bone-dry. They never learned how it got there.

The fire, caused by faulty wiring in an old refrigerator in the basement, had destroyed nearly all of my parents' material possessions. Trying to "find the good" in the midst of that reality, Dad had joked, "At least there won't be much for you guys to fight about after we are gone." And this proved to be true. But at the time, and later, we reflected on the symbolic significance of the few items that survived the fire. The photographs helped us recall our youth and remember the importance of family. The nativity set and wedding prayer book were tangible proof of my parents' spirituality and religious beliefs, which we, their children, now try to pass on to our own children. And every Christmas since the fire, as we hang those ten stockings, we are reminded of the grandmother who made them.

The coincidences surrounding the fire were thin-place experiences that taught each of us to look for the good, even in the most difficult situations. The lingering lessons of the fire encouraged us to detach from "stuff" and be grateful for all that we have. Since that day, the love and happiness once contained within the walls of the old house have expanded into ten more households. The good feelings emerge often, whenever we gather as a clan that now numbers more than fifty. I can still hear my mother's voice calling me as a teenager, as I would back out of the driveway with a car full of siblings. "Be careful, honey," she'd say. "You have my most precious possessions in that car!" As we all faced the aftermath of Dad's death, more than ever we still were Mom's most precious possessions. All the rest was just stuff.

The coincidence of finding the funeral card and letters that survived the fire taught me to pay even closer attention to the coincidences in my life, the thin-place times when God sends us important messages. And, after listening to so many similar stories from others, it does seem that the more we pay attention, the more frequently the coincidences occur. Maybe God realizes "They get it—finally!" and then continues to communicate to us in ways we are increasingly able to comprehend. The funeral card incident became the first of several coincidences that my siblings and I observed over the next few months.

Chapter Twelve

LOVE AS A THIN PLACE

> When we come to the last moment of
> this lifetime, and we look back across it,
> the only thing that's going to matter is
> "What was the quality of our love?"
>
> —RICHARD BACH

LATE MARCH 2002

Toward the end of March, Beth and I met at her church late one evening to spend an hour in prayer together. We had not seen each other for a couple of weeks, although we had spoken several times by phone. Our time together was spent in silence, which wasn't easy for two chatty people. Beth prays like this once a week; I come whenever I can. It is a profound spiritual ritual for both of us, one that we continue to this day. This time spent in prayer together is unique among my friendships, and is a key component of my deeper soul friendship with Beth.

As usual, Beth arrived before me, and was now seated in a small room at the end of a "gathering space" adjacent to the sanctuary where Mass is said. Stained-glass doors adorn the entrance to a half-moon-shaped chapel. Here, the only furnishings are benches and kneelers. In the center of the room, a marble stand is topped with a gold monstrance, a star-shaped container with a glass center that contains a single consecrated communion host. In many Catholic churches, a room like this allows parishioners to spend one hour a week engaged in a tradition called "perpetual eucharistic adoration."

I silently prayed the rosary, using plastic beads apparently made by a thoughtful parishioner and left outside the chapel for people who did not bring their own rosary. The rest of my hour was spent in the meditative practice of centering prayer, which concluded with reading a daily devotional-type book called God Calling. Another good friend gave me this book many years ago, and I gave a copy to Beth. We both find the daily readings often contain a message that presents itself exactly when we need to hear it most. Since I have begun this practice of spending this weekly hour in silent prayer and reflection, life has been more peaceful, less worrisome. Spending our hour of silent prayer together leaves me more aware of the moments of grace within the thin-place experiences in my life.

After the hour of silence, Beth and I walked together to our cars and visited for awhile about our Easter vacation trips with our families. I told her about my week on the Gulf of Mexico with Maureen, Emmy, and John, together with our families and Paul, in rental condos overlooking the white sand of Gulf Shores, Alabama. It was the perfect place to spend Easter vacation; my parents had loved traveling there and encouraged us to bring our own families to the area. All efforts to persuade Mom to join us this time had been futile, however. She told us it would have been too hard to return there without Dad.

Instead, she traveled to Kansas City with Molly's family to spend Easter with Dennis and Julie and their family. Molly drove Mom and Molly's two youngest in one car; her husband, George, drove the rest of their brood in another. During the eight-hour drive, Mom listened to the audiotape of Dad's funeral; it was the first time she had heard the recording. The actual funeral had been a blur for Mom, so she was grateful to hear the music, readings, and sentimental tributes again.

Molly told us later that during the drive Mom admitted she finally had read about her disease, idiopathic pulmonary fibrosis. When she was first diagnosed, it was Dad who got on the Internet sites recommended by Kevin to learn more about the disease. As he researched IPF, Dad shared that information with the rest of us. As one would expect, reading about his wife's dire prognosis was upsetting for Dad. Mom did not want to know the details or prognosis. She chose not to read about IPF, except to learn what she needed to do to begin treating her disease.

We all knew she was in denial, but also realized this was her way of maintaining a positive attitude. Long before the interconnectedness of the mental, emotional, and spiritual dimensions of illness became better appreciated, we, as youngsters, had frequently heard one of Mom's favorite one-liners, "Mind over matter." And if she could do nothing about the "matter," well, she simply would deal with it in her own way: to live as fully as she could and not worry about the future. Now, with Dad gone, she no longer needed to put up a positive front to make her illness easier for anyone else to accept, especially him. Mom also was becoming more realistic about the difficulties of life without Dad and the seriousness of her disease. After reading the information about IPF, she said to Molly that she "didn't realize how fatal it was." For the first time, she acknowledged that she might not live until Paul's ordination.

Some of us wondered if the stark realization of her terminal prognosis would cause Mom to give up, to forgo the drugs that might stabilize her condition. Molly noticed she took lots of naps at Dennis's house. Soon after the Easter trip, Mom's condition deteriorated rapidly. Perhaps there was a connection, but I couldn't imagine her giving up. Perhaps she simply wore herself out helping her husband die. During Dad's final weeks of life, Mom kept saying how she was receiving the grace she needed to help him. Maybe so. But looking back, I think she was far sicker than she let on.

On Monday, April 8, I was once again at Mom's house, going through "the stuff." We had several of these special times. On this particular day, another significant survivor of the fire emerged. Mom sat on a red leather chair in the office next to Dad's desk. She was sifting through a box of file folders while I sat on the floor surrounded by a half-filled black trash bag. I silently wondered why we had not finished this little project by now, since some of my siblings had also spent several days decluttering the rest of the house, but our plodding thoroughness was about to be rewarded. Near the bottom of this day's bag, I discovered an envelope filled with twelve pages from a yellow-lined tablet. The edges were rimmed with the telltale black tinge that meant it too had survived the fire.

The pages were filled with Mom's handwriting. Holding up the pages, I asked if she knew what it was. She didn't until I read a few lines that appeared to be the opening statement of a speech. "Oh, I remember that," she exclaimed. "That's a speech I gave back in 1966 to students at St. Joseph Academy"—a now-closed Catholic girls high school in St. Paul. "The topic was the importance of family relation-ships," she added. "Your Great-Aunt Vera asked me to speak to a class she was teaching."

"Well, that was a compliment. She must have thought you did a good job with raising our family," I commented.

"I guess so. You all turned out pretty well."

"Would if be OK if I took it home and read it later, Mom?"

"Absolutely. Take it with you."

As with Dad's letter to Gongie, Mom no longer wanted to save anything for herself—even personal papers like these. Or maybe, knowing the seriousness of her illness, she wanted to begin distribut-ing these items so we would have them after she was gone. Mom was not particularly sentimental. She was kind and thoughtful, but also pragmatic and practical. I was a bit surprised she had kept even this speech, unless she thought she could use it again sometime.

I was excited to find this rare remnant of my mother's brief career as a public speaker, but I also found that the timing was interesting. For nearly forty years, the twelve pages had laid in an envelope on the bottom of a fireproof file cabinet that had served its purpose when the house burned down. Coincidentally, I found her speech less than a week before I was to give a similar speech at a parish retreat for moth-ers and grandmothers. My topic was "Mothers as Spiritual Directors," and I planned to include a discussion of the spiritual dimension of family relationships. After reading Mom's speech later that evening,

I called to ask if she would mind if I used some of her words in my talk the following Saturday. She was flattered.

I had given similar talks, but Mom had never seen me speak publicly. For some reason, perhaps because of the topic, I especially wanted her to be present at this one. Maureen and Emmy invited her to attend the one-day retreat, held at their (and my former) parish, St. Joseph's Catholic Church in West St. Paul. I felt like a kid, seeking her approval, hoping I could convey adequately some of the lessons she had taught me so well.

My talk was scheduled to be the first one after lunch. While the two morning speakers gave their talks, I kept looking for Mom to arrive, but she did not. This did not surprise me. She had seemed tired recently, so I thought perhaps she had decided to sleep in. When it was time to break for lunch, she still had not arrived. I was beginning to worry, as did my sisters.

We all went into the parish school lunchroom, navigated through a buffet line, and sat with our meals. About ten minutes later, Mom appeared in the doorway and walked, almost shuffling, toward us. One of my sisters jumped up to show her where we were seated. Mom grinned as we made room for her. "Sorry I'm late," she said. "I'm moving slowly today." We all must have been in denial regarding the severity of her illness. In denial herself, she was determined to remain independent and refused to let one of us pick her up and drive her to the event.

"Don't worry about it, Mom," I said, relieved. "We're just glad you're here."

Returning to the church sanctuary, where the retreat was being held, Mom sat with Maureen and Emmy. I began my talk, which encouraged mothers and grandmothers to help their children and grandchildren find God in their lives. Near the end of my speech, I mentioned that my mother was present and that my closing words actually were the ones she had written nearly thirty-five years earlier. I then held up the worn yellow pages with the burn-tinged edges and told the audience how the papers should have burned in our house fire, but did not. Before reading Mom's text, without realizing it, I said a dumb but strangely prophetic thing: At some point in my talk, I had meant to refer to my mother as a "dear soul." Instead, I said,

"My mother, God rest her soul." Emmy told me later that after hearing my faux pas, Mom leaned over and whispered, "She's got me in the grave already," which got my sisters giggling. Fortunately, I did not realize my gaffe and concluded with one of the final paragraphs from Mom's speech:

> If I were to leave you with one simple thought on how to get the most out of life within your present families and later when you have your own, I would have to tell you to learn to be lovers in the full sense of the word. With love you can do almost anything. Without it, life at any stage can be miserable. By loving, you give of yourself, and the more you can give, the greater will you enjoy and be enjoyed. There is no absolute formula on how to raise a perfect family, but from the time we are infants we learn to love out of our dependence on our parents. Through the love for our parents we learn to love God. So we begin, one step at a time, to learn to love others and to delight in being loved. We are secure in our parents' love and in God's love and we learn to return love to both of them.

While I prepared my talk, Mom's words reminded me of the many things she had done to manifest her love for others. She had not only written about loving others, she had lived those words. She was not one to sit and visit for long periods of time, unlike Dad, who liked to just "be," holding court from his recliner. Mom was much happier "doing something," not only for her family, but for friends, neighbors, and students at the high school where she was a substitute teacher. She baked banana bread for new neighbors and made baby blankets for pregnant high school students, never judging their condition. We would learn, after her death, that when she once heard about a student who could not afford a trip with the school band, she gave the principal four hundred dollars so the young man could go. Quietly, often anonymously, Mom had been a channel of God's love, to her family and others she cared about. In doing so, she responded to the nudge God sends us to be thin places to each other, to be the vehicle for people to feel God's love.

After reading her words of wisdom to the audience, I looked at Mom and thanked her for teaching me how to love others. I had never thanked her for that before. I'm glad I did so then, for within three weeks she was gone.

Chapter Thirteen

THE ABSENCE OF THIN PLACES

The Lord is my shepherd; I shall not want.
He makes me lie down in green pastures.
He leads me besides still waters; he restores my
    soul.
He leads me in paths of righteousness for his
    name's sake.
Even though I walk through the valley of the
    shadow of death, I fear no evil;
For thou art with me; thy rod and thy staff,
    they comfort me.
Thou preparest a table before me in the pres-
    ence of my enemies;
Thou anointest my head with oil, my cup over-
    flows.
Surely goodness and mercy shall follow me all
    the days of my life;
And I shall dwell in the house of the Lord for
    ever.

—PSALM 23 (RSV)

APRIL 17, 2002

The grief of losing Dad left my heart heavy, both for myself and for Mom. During the first few weeks after he died, I felt sad that I didn't notice any thin-place experiences. Thin places would not be evident to me until the last few days of Mom's life. I'm not sure if this was because there were none or because I wasn't looking for them, or because I was too dazed to be aware of them. Most days were a blur, filled with the routines of daily life.

One routine proved to be especially therapeutic: my frequent conversations with Beth. Now with the earlier spring daylight, we resurrected our tradition of almost daily walks at sunrise. "How was your mother yesterday?" she asked as I sat on the stoop outside my mudroom door and tightened the laces on a well-worn pair of walking shoes.

"Not herself at all," I replied. "I'm really worried about her."

"Is her physical condition worsening, or is it her grief that has you concerned?"

"Both. She's worn down emotionally and physically, yet she pushes herself to stay busy and maintain the routine she had with Dad. Like yesterday morning: She was adamant about going to Mass. Frankly, I hate the idea of her getting up at 5:30 and driving half an hour to get to church by 7:00. We're trying to convince her that God does not expect her to risk her own health if it becomes too difficult for her to attend Mass. But this has been her daily ritual for most of her life. I think now her religion is more important to her than ever."

"And your mom's physical health?" Beth asked.

"She seems to be getting worse by the day. And her appetite is next to nothing."

"That could also be due to the grief, you know."

"I'm sure you're right. But I also wonder about her mental and emotional health." When Mom and I had gone to breakfast after Mass the day before, I commented on her lack of appetite. She said she wasn't very hungry, saying, "We old folks don't need much."

We all were worried about Mom's condition after we realized she had no memory of an hour-long drive later that day. Nurse Molly knew Mom's sudden lack of memory could mean she was oxygen-deprived. After a trip to the hospital, the doctors validated my sister's concern and sent Mom home with an oxygen tank. The oxygen helped restore her mental capabilities and she seemed to improve. Paul offered to stay with her over the weekend. He was surprised when Mom, an avid reader, told him she couldn't get into a book, so he offered to rent a movie "to take your mind off things." They spent the evening watching K-Pax. It would be their last Friday mother-son date.

After the movie ended, Mom began rolling up the cord to her oxygen machine as she prepared to go upstairs to bed. When Paul leaned over to kiss her goodnight, she whispered, "I told Father Malone and the doctors that I need to make it to your ordination. They just have to get me four more years."

"I know you'll be there one way or another, Mom," Paul said. "I'm not worried. Besides, it's only four more years."

Still looking down at the cord, she nodded her head and said, "Thanks, Paul. Good night. Love ya."

"Love you too, Mom."

As Paul watched her leave the room, he suddenly understood the gravity of her condition. Later, he shared with our family the realization that, "for the first time, I told her that it would be all right if she was with me in spirit at my ordination. She seemed to appreciate that permission."

The next morning, Mom didn't get up at her usual early hour. By ten o'clock, she still hadn't come downstairs. Paul knocked on her door, peeked his head in her room, and asked, "Mom, are you OK?" She said she felt lousy. It was the first time Paul ever heard her admit she was sick. Nausea—a probable side effect of her medication—had kept her up during the night, and she still needed to rest. She stayed in bed until early afternoon. Shuffling into the living room in her pajamas, she sank into a recliner and said, "I can't ever remember feeling this miserable." Concerned, Paul stayed with her all day and canceled his evening plans. Ordinarily, she would have told him not to worry and to go home, but this time she simply said, "Great." She headed back to bed until early evening, when she and Paul watched another movie together.

APRIL 21, 2002

On Sunday morning, Mom felt worse. Paul called Molly, who convinced Mom that she needed to go to the emergency room. Despite her insistence that her medication side effects were the problem, Mom agreed to go. She and Paul got to the hospital around noon; Molly arrived soon after. After Mom was admitted and helped into a bed, she told Molly, Paul, and the medical resident that she was so miserable, she "felt like dying." All denials and mind-over-matter rhetoric were gone. The only thing she could talk about was how nauseated she felt. Her legs were twitching too, a symptom of the restless-leg condition she had had for years. Molly gently rubbed them as they waited for the doctor to examine Mom. As he took her medical history, Molly and Paul added details and corrections. When the resident asked, "Is there anything else?" Mom was silent.

"Yes," Molly said. "She just lost her husband."

Hearing this, Mom fell apart. Paul told us later that he had not seen her cry like that since he walked into Dad's room at the hospice and saw her lying over his body, sobbing. Paul had wrapped his arms around her and cried with her. Now, the raised metal bars on either side of her bed kept him at arm's length. Molly and Paul described for the doctor the losses Mom had endured over the past few months: her health, her job, her sister, her husband, and soon the home she and Dad had shared for decades. The stark reality of how Mom's life had changed so dramatically must have intensified the physical pain she now felt. Watching her suffer was heartbreaking for my sister and brother.

All of us had thought Mom's deteriorating health was a reaction to her medicine, or that she had caught a flu bug and was dehydrated. She seemed to know better, because something had recently prompted her to ask Maureen (who tracked her finances): "Are all my affairs in order?"

Monday evening, the doctors advised us that Mom's frail body was filled with infection. She was in septic shock and her kidneys were shutting down. By the time the rest of the in-town siblings gathered at the hospital, she was on dialysis. Numbed by the news, we sat together in the family lounge, waiting for an update on her condition, wondering how this could be happening again so soon after Dad's death. We had just been in this room, at this hospital, waiting for news about Dad.

For a while, the dialysis treatment stabilized Mom's condition, and she was moved to a floor where she would be closely monitored. We visited briefly with her. She still was in pain, and not shy about letting us know it. Until then, I had rarely heard her complain about anything. But that was Mom. At other times in her life, her unwillingness to admit she was sick had resulted in her condition worsening. When we traveled (via a station wagon hitched to a trailer this time) to the Washington, D.C., area to visit Dad's sister Pat and her family over Christmas in 1965, Mom was sick the entire trip. She had a bad cough and it got worse by the day. She was nearly seven months' pregnant, and didn't yet know she was expecting twins. She kept telling us she just had a cold. Dad finally insisted she see a doctor when we arrived at my aunt's home. Mom had severe pneumonia.

This time, she had become so sick, so quickly. The infection erupted like wildfire throughout her body, resisting treatment. We learned later that she was fortunate to have survived that Monday night. We were allowed brief visits with her, while the doctors fought to save her. Mom was in pain and, I suspect, afraid. She coughed violently and had trouble breathing. Still, as my siblings and I took turns sitting in the visitors lobby, I felt angry at Mom. Why hadn't she let us know sooner how awful she was feeling? I also felt guilty for not having been more perceptive. All we could do now was wait and pray we would not lose her too.

We left around 2:00 A.M., hopeful that her condition would improve, telling her that we would see her the following day. We each hugged her and told her we loved her, knowing from our experience with Dad how important it was to say the words as often as possible, in case we might not have another chance. The doctor on duty had warned us she might have to insert a ventilator if Mom was having too much difficulty breathing. We thought the ventilator would be a temporary necessity. Several of us were present when the doctor asked Mom if she would consent to this procedure. Her response indicated her will to live: "Sure, why wouldn't I?" We knew Mom wouldn't be able to talk if she were on a ventilator. What we didn't know is that she would also be unconscious.

The next morning, the doctor on duty called Molly at home to let her know that Mom was likely to be put on the ventilator. Molly raced over to the hospital, but they had already intubated Mom. The nurse assured our sister that Mom had been lucid before the tube was put down her throat, and had understood that the ventilator was the only way she would be able to breathe more easily. The nurse said Mom accepted this, and seemed relatively calm. All of us felt bad, and still feel bad, that we weren't able to see Mom or be with her before she was rendered unconscious. But we also knew that the doctors did what they deemed necessary to try to save her life.

In the midst of our grief for Dad, we were fearing the worst for Mom. When the event you most dread becomes imminent, it can be hard to look for the thin places, where God is present in the midst of mayhem. But even in the worst of times, signs can and do appear to console us. In our case, sometimes when we didn't notice them at first, they would appear again and again and again, confirming my belief that things that come in threes might somehow be divinely inspired.

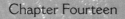

Chapter Fourteen

ANGELIC THIN PLACES

One of the things we easily forget
while in the depths of pain is to look
for the Holy. We are simply preoccu-
pied with daily survival. But sometimes the Holy sneaks up on us, in
ways that surprise us, like the gentle
caring word from a nurse, and angel-
like appearance in a therapist's office,
a word from scripture that sustains us,
the appearance of a friend we haven't
seen for years, or a bird that will not
leave our window sill. These little
things help us make it through the day
or a week and help us see that we are
not alone or forgotten.

—JANET O. HAGBERG

APRIL 23, 2002

By late morning, the seven in-town siblings
were gathered at the hospital, along with sev-
eral of our spouses. The out-of-towners—
Sheila in Portland, Dennis in Kansas City, Kevin in
Duluth—each got there as soon as he or she could.
With each sibling's arrival to the lounge, fresh tears

fell as we hugged each other tightly. When Beth came to the lounge around 6:00 that evening, I missed seeing her because I was in Mom's room. As usual, Beth knew what to do: Dropping off a platter of meats, cheese, sandwich rolls, and dessert bars, she quickly left after hugging my sisters, not wanting to intrude by staying too long.

In the crowded lounge, we struggled with roller-coaster emotions. One moment we felt angry and bitter at the unfairness of it all, the next we felt stunned. Even on that horrible day, we could still laugh. A brief burst of inappropriate Treacy humor lifted the sadness when someone said, "Thank God Dad isn't here to see this. It would kill him."

Doctors had given us some hope that Mom would recover, but it was slim. Even if she did recover, what condition would she be in? Would she be able to breathe on her own? Would she have suffered brain damage? While the rest of us grappled with fears of the unknown, Paul said, "We'll take her however we get her." Hearing this, I silently prayed. *Please God, don't take her. I cannot bear to think of life without both of my parents. Not this close together. Not yet.*

Our mother was alive, but I think most of us knew we were about to become orphaned. *Orphaned.* It's a strange word to describe ten middle-aged adults between the ages of thirty-six and forty-nine, but that's how we felt. Thank God we had each other, our spouses, and our children.

As word spread of my mother's perilous condition, visitors began to arrive. Among the first was our parish priest, Father Malone, who had been so good to us during Dad's illness. He was dressed in street clothes, and his expression conveyed immediate sympathy. All of us rose to hug him, shedding more tears. As I waited for him to speak, I suddenly felt detached from the room, looking at the situation as a spiritual director rather than a daughter of a woman near death. For a moment, I was curious to see how another spiritual counselor would tend to the needs of so many people at once. What pastoral skills would he draw on to guide us? He would never suggest this was God's will. What could he possibly say to comfort us?

What Father Malone offered on that difficult day was simply his presence, along with a few comforting words of wisdom. He listened as we told him of our anxiety and despair, of our dismay at not being with Mom before the ventilator was inserted into her throat. We had treasured the many "grace of a happy death" bedside conversations with our father—times when we told him how much he meant to us. Where was that grace now? If only just one of us could have shared our feelings with Mom before she became unconscious. If only we had paid more attention to how sick she really had been. I had other regrets: *If only I had more time to get to know her, out of the shadow of Dad's immense presence—then perhaps she would have known how much she too had meant to me.*

After a pause in the conversation, Father Malone spoke. "I know you wish you could have reassured your mother that you loved her and told her how important she was to you," he said. "But you already did say those things to her. When you all thanked your dad and said good-bye to him, you also thanked your mother. She knew how much she meant to you because you said that to both your parents, not just your father." He was right. In nearly every conversation we had with Dad, Mom had been present. The memories and stories we shared with him often included her. When we thanked him and expressed our love for him every night before we left him, we had conveyed these same sentiments to our mother.

Father Malone also addressed our other big concern, saying it was possible Mom might never be able to breathe on her own without a ventilator. As the infection destroyed her body, and the doctors determined there was nothing more they could do to save her, we would have to decide whether to take her off the ventilator. "Look at this from your mother's perspective," he said as he looked at our stricken faces. "What would she want? You already know your mother's wishes regarding her end-of-life care." This also was true. One of the many blessings during Dad's final days had been his willingness to declare his wishes regarding his death. He and Mom both had living wills; they did not want extraordinary efforts to keep them alive if there was no chance of recovery.

Father Malone's words brought great comfort, confirming what we already knew: that our parents' strong faith had prepared them for this moment because we had discussed it with them. I had grown to appreciate the religion of my youth much more during Dad's illness and death. Now I felt grateful for the compassion that this priest and friend was offering to our family when we most needed it. I felt at peace for the first time since Mom had been admitted. All would be well, even if my mother did not survive.

After several hours, we were told that Mom's condition had stabilized, although she was not yet out of the woods. And so began the long wait. On this first day of her induced coma, all of us, including the doctor, still felt optimistic that she might survive this crisis. We decided to tend to our normal lives for a while, making sure at least two of us were always at the hospital. Thanks to cell phones, everyone could be reached anywhere at any time.

From the hospital, I went to the high school in St. Paul where my youngest two children were students. Midterm conferences were being held that afternoon, and although I certainly could have skipped them, I needed a break from the intensity of the hospital experience. Molly, Maureen, and Emmy also had children there and came to conferences that afternoon and evening. Only later did I realize that what I craved that afternoon at the school conference was a sense of community, a place where friends would comfort me. I hadn't seen some of these friends and acquaintances since Dad's funeral. When they asked how I was coping with his death, then learned about Mom's condition, they were shocked. Several who had known my parents for years got teary at the news. Yet their expressions of sympathy were nurturing, and the promises of prayers were welcomed. I left the school feeling uplifted by the support I had just received.

Dan and I returned to the hospital that evening, and again the next morning. Dan stopped in frequently, as did all of the spouses. Several siblings always were present throughout the day, taking breaks when needed, returning to children and jobs only to check in. I think we all realized there was no place we would rather be together than near our mother, knowing we likely would never have this time with her again.

The doctors did a superb job of updating us, but within a couple of days after Mom was put on the ventilator, we began to lose hope. We realized she might be in a coma for an extended period of time—and this would not help her prospects for long-term survival. Dennis needed to get back to his own family in Kansas City, but he didn't want to leave before he had some sort of sign that Mom could hear him, some gesture that would leave him with hope she might recover. He just wanted a blink or a squeeze of her hand, anything to reassure him.

On Saturday, he got his wish.

We were told of a drug the doctors could give Mom that would bring her out of the coma for a few minutes, when she might be able to hear and perhaps understand us. As a family, we decided to have the drug administered while Dennis was still in town. We all wanted him to get his sign from Mom before he left town. We also had been told there might be other times when Mom could be brought out of the coma, so we held onto the hope that each of us would be able to speak with her later.

Dennis asked if I would come with him during his time with Mom. "Absolutely," I told him, touched by his request. We entered Mom's room with trepidation and curiosity about might happen. Our mother had been unconscious for five days. Was it really possible she could be brought out of the coma? Would she really be able to hear us, and understand what we were saying? Or would she be in a vegetative state, unable to communicate with us ever again? But seconds after the drug was put into her IV line, Mom opened her eyes slightly, startling both of us. Her deep brown eyes were cloudy and unfocused. Dennis and I stood on either side of the bed, holding her hands. We took turns speaking, reassuring her that everyone was here, that we were praying for her, and that we all loved her very much. I explained that Dennis had to return soon to Kansas City and he wanted just a squeeze from her hand, so he could continue to be hopeful about her recovery.

"Mom, could you please try to squeeze Dennis's hand, just a bit, so he will know you hear us?" I never thought to mention that he was on her right side, and I was on her left. I felt a slight tug as she weakly squeezed my palm. "Whoops—Mom, thank you for that sign. But Dennis is on your right side. Do you think you can turn your head toward him?"

Almost immediately, she did. My brother and I were overjoyed. Knowing this moment wouldn't last, we showered her with words of love, affection, and gratitude, speaking for all of our siblings as well as ourselves. She couldn't reply, of course, but we knew our words had been heard. What a gift it was. Then, all too soon, her eyes closed, and she was again unresponsive. Dennis and I held each other and cried. After composing ourselves a bit, we returned to the lounge where the rest of the family waited. That we were able to connect with Mom comforted everyone. It confirmed for all of us that her mind was functioning, despite the coma. We would continue speaking to her, knowing there was a good chance she could hear us.

A day or two later, while cleaning and vacuuming her car at the gas station, Maureen noticed something shiny on the carpet near the back seat. It appeared to be a plain silver coin. Turning the coin over, she discovered that the other side had an angel carved on it. A *guardian angel*, Maureen thought, *just like Mom always told us about.* When Maureen told us the coin story at the hospital the next day, I couldn't believe it: I had found the same type of coin that same morning. Like Maureen, I also found it while vacuuming the car. Memories of Mom and angels flooded my mind. When we would leave the house every morning for the mile-long walk to school, she would stand at the door and say the same words every day: "May your guardian angel watch over you today and keep you safe." Each of us had our own angel, Mom told us, and they (and various saints) were my mother's spiritual friends. Any good thing that happened to us—whether it was protection from fender benders, recoveries from serious illness (as when Emmy was fifteen and almost died from toxic-shock infection), or safe cross-country journeys—she attributed it to the benevolence of our guardian angels.

Mom was a strong believer in the power of intercessory prayer as well. If she needed a special favor, she talked to the saints, asking them to speak to God on our behalf. Certain saints received certain requests. If she lost something, for example, she asked St. Anthony to help her find it. And both Mom and Dad claimed it was their prayers to St. Joseph that helped sell all their homes quickly on their own. My non-Catholic friends (and some Catholics as well) think these practices are a bit strange, but I must admit that Mom's prayer rituals often worked. Her conversation with St. Anthony seemed to help when I lost a contact lens during an amorous evening with Dan on the grounds of the College of St. Catherine, my alma mater. The next day, I went back to the scene of our date, with Mom kneeling on the grass with me. After saying three Apostle's Creeds and praying to God through St. Anthony, she found the lens. "Here it is," she said triumphantly. "St. Anthony does it again!" As much as I once mocked Mom for this ritual, I can't think of a time when such petitions *didn't* work for her, although we probably wouldn't have heard about it. And they've worked for me too, as I've found numerous lost items (including another contact lens, under football bleachers, *at night*) after asking St. Anthony for help.

For bigger challenges, Mom said novenas—a series of prayers to a particular saint prayed over nine consecutive days. Taped to the mirror in Mom's bathroom was a picture of her favorite saint, St. Therese of Lisieux. In her autobiography, *Story of a Soul*, this Carmelite nun wrote that she would "do more good [than she did on earth] from heaven." As she was dying, Therese promised to intercede on the behalf of others once she was in heaven. "It will be like a shower of roses," she said. "After my death, you will go to the mail box, and you will find many consolations." We would receive signs that validated Mom's unwavering belief in intercessory prayer a few weeks later.

We marveled at the coincidence of finding the coins. Why had Maureen and I performed such a trivial task during such a traumatic time? I suggested we should watch for a third appearance of an angel coin, affirming my belief in divine messages coming as a trio of signs. We didn't have to wait long. The next day, when I stopped in the hospital gift shop, the first thing I saw was a basketful of angel coins identical to the ones Maureen and I had found.

The appearance of the angel coins boosted our spirits. *Maybe Mom would pull out of this. Maybe she could recover from the infection that was ravaging her fragile body. Maybe she would live to see Paul ordained.* But even the angels could not produce a medical miracle for our mother. During the final days of her life, however, we did receive comfort and love from human angels. Friends and neighbors delivered food to the hospital lounge and to our homes and drove our kids to after-school activities. My parents' longtime friends— "the Irish Mafia," as they call themselves—sent artificial flowers when they learned that real flowers weren't allowed in the intensive care unit. Sheila's good friend since high school, Mag (a physical therapist like Sheila), gave shoulder and neck massages to anyone who needed a stress reliever. Visitors like Mag who had recently lost a parent whispered words of encouragement only they completely understood. Mom's in-town siblings, their spouses, and some of our cousins sat with Mom and with us, sharing stories and sometimes laughter. Father Malone, Father Steve (the hospital chaplain), and Archbishop Flynn prayed with us. So many angels, including Mom's nurses and doctors, cared for us during this devastating time. Through their acts of love and kindness, both large and small, they were truly channels of God's mercy and grace. In their presence, one of the most difficult times in our lives became a thin-place experience.

A few months later, another angel coin appeared, sustaining our hope in a heaven where souls abide with angels and affirming our belief in the presence of angels here on earth. The coin appeared when our sister Emmy found it under the passenger-side seat of the family car, which had been in an accident. Her oldest daughter was driving; Emmy's son and Maureen's two children were passengers. The children received only minor injuries in the crash. The car was nearly demolished.

Chapter Fifteen

PRAYER AS A THIN PLACE

THE PRAYER OF AN UNKNOWN CONFEDERATE SOLDIER

I asked God for strength that I might achieve;
I was made weak that I might learn to obey.

I asked for health that I might do great things;
I was given infirmity that I might do better things.

I asked for riches that I might be happy;
I was given poverty that I might be wise.

I asked for power that I might have the praise
of men;
I was given weakness that I might feel the
need of God.

I asked for all things that I might enjoy life;
I was given life that I might enjoy all things.

I got nothing that I had asked for,
But everything that I had hoped for.

Almost despite myself my unspoken prayers
were answered;
I am, among all men, most richly blessed.

LATE APRIL 2002

As during Dad's hospitalization, our family received cards, letters, and e-mail during Mom's final days. Many arrived with messages of people praying for us. Once again, our family could sense the prayers of others. Being the recipients of prayers created a thin place that was both safe and sacred, where we hoped for a miracle and yet also prepared for what would happen without one. I sometimes wonder if certain people have special pipelines to God because their lives seem to be prayers in themselves. Just being with them makes you feel as though God has sent them directly to you, in answer to your pleas for help.

Mom's sister, the first-born of Leo and Leone Culligan's eight children, is one of those people. Aunt Mary's presence fills a room with peacefulness and love. She drove with her husband, Dave, from their home in northern Indiana as soon as they heard about Mom's hospitalization. When she arrived at the hospital, it was as if Mom was with us again, hugging us and sharing words of comfort. Aunt Mary was a year older than Mom; the two of them could have been twins, they looked and talked so much alike.

For the next few days, Aunt Mary was with Mom almost constantly. From the moment she entered Mom's room, she began speaking softly to her with absolute confidence that her words would be heard. Her presence was as reassuring to us as it must have been to her little sister. As she gently stroked my mother's thin white hair, Aunt Mary placed her head next to Mom's ear and told her how much everyone loved her, and how much Jesus loved her. "You are so close to Jesus," she whispered, telling Mom she would be fine, no matter what happened. Other times, our aunt would alternately hold Mom's hand and softly rub her arm as her lips moved in silent prayer.

When she was not with Mom, Aunt Mary was ministering to us, and I no longer felt like an orphan. She was with the family on Sunday, April 29, to witness an extraordinary moment. Dan and I had visited Mom that afternoon, then left for the theater, thinking her condition was stable enough that we could be gone for a few hours. Dan and our children had understood my need to spend as much time as I could at the hospital. He and I had our time for "pillow talk" (Mom's oft-used phrase) every morning, but at night I was often too exhausted, both physically and emotionally, to visit with him for more than a few minutes. Dan and I looked forward to dinner and a night alone with each other. I don't think I told my siblings much more than that we were going to dinner and a play. Entering the theater, I turned off my cell phone.

As Dan and I watched the antics of the actors performing *The Canterbury Tales*, Mom was having another health crisis. Her blood pressure dropped to 34/10 and stayed there. The situation was grave. Emmy suggested that everyone pray together. As Mom's condition deteriorated, the rosary was recited around her bedside. In the middle of saying the rosary, Mom's blood pressure went up, along with the oxygen levels in her blood. The nurse noticed the dramatic change and commented, "Either it's your prayers that have caused this little miracle or I'm a very good nurse!"

This was to be a short-term reprieve, yet several of my siblings interpreted Mom's temporary improvement after all the prayers as a significant coincidence. It was as if Mom was rallying to live in response to hearing her children say the rosary. It would be just like her to want to show us how prayers really do help. She certainly had preached that lesson to us all our lives. The memory of this event still serves to reaffirm what she taught us about the importance of prayer.

The next few days were a blur of conflicting medical reports about Mom's condition. She was deteriorating again, and quickly. The doctors warned us that we soon would be faced with the decision of whether to remove the ventilator.

What could be more devastating than having to decide to remove life support from a loved one? How could we just let our mother go? How would we ever know if recovery was possible? How could we know that there might not be a miracle? Speaking for myself, I wanted someone else to make this decision. But the only one who could do so without feeling guilty was in a coma, relying on her children to decide.

As Father Malone had reminded us, Mom had left clear guidance for us. By signing a living will, she made it clear that she didn't want to be kept alive by extraordinary means. We knew this, but deciding which means are extraordinary and which are lifesaving is not easy. It was also important to all of us that our decision be consistent with the teachings of our religion, since that consideration would have been crucial to both our parents.

Mom's doctors did not rush us. Because we needed their professional assessment of her prognosis, we decided we would include her family doctor in a meeting the next morning. We shared our feelings about this important decision as Mom's condition worsened by the moment. Just before we left, someone suggested we pray and ask God to guide us with this momentous decision: "God, please grant all of us the wisdom to know what to do tomorrow. We ask that you be with us, especially tonight and tomorrow, to guide us with what we need to do. Amen."

APRIL 30

The next morning, the in-town siblings gathered in the hospital conference room. Dennis, Sheila, and Kevin participated via speakerphone. When the doctor entered and looked at each of us, I felt sympathy for the man. I wondered if his task of helping families make life-or-death decisions got any easier with time. He sat at the head of the table, and began to assure us that every possible medical procedure had been done. When asked about Mom's chances for surviving without the ventilator, he said, "Probably less than 10 percent."

As a physician, Kevin asked all the appropriate medical questions we wouldn't have known to ask. He wanted to be certain no other treatment options existed for Mom. I was grateful for his thorough discussion with the doctor. "Even with the very slim chance of your mother's ability to survive this crisis," he told us, "she must still deal with her IPF disease. Think of it as if we asked her to climb one mountain only to put another, bigger mountain in front of her and tell her, 'OK, now you must overcome this huge obstacle too.'" The doctor would leave the decision up to us, but his prognosis left little doubt about Mom's chances for recovery.

At first, no one spoke. We had agreed that our decision must be unanimous; if anyone was uncomfortable with turning off the ventilator, it would not be done. But one by one, we said what was in our hearts, and soon we agreed that we wanted to honor both our parents' wishes: The ventilator would be removed. Some of us thought once the decision was made, the machine would be turned off that day. Many of us had prepared ourselves, but others were not ready. We decided to wait until everyone was in the same place—mentally, emotionally, and spiritually—with what we were about to do.

MAY 1

The next morning, my brother Dennis prayed to receive some affirmation that this was the right decision. He and his wife, Julie, drove to their local parish church in Kansas City. The school choir, practicing for an upcoming Mass, was singing "Down to the River to Pray," the song our father loved, the one that was played at his funeral. Dennis said later that hearing this song validated our decision. "It felt like Dad was sending a sign to say, 'It's time for Mom to leave you. But she will be with me soon. Don't be sad.'" There were other indications that letting Mom go on this day was the right thing to do. After the service, when Dennis asked about the intention for the Mass, he was told, "It is to honor teachers." Mom was a teacher. In the Catholic faith, May 1 is a day to honor St. Joseph the Worker, the patron saint who helps people die a peaceful death. May 1 is also a day to honor the Blessed Virgin.

Mom would have loved the spiritual significance of what would be her last day alive. We planned a special ritual for saying our final good-byes. Father Malone was out of town, so we asked Father Jim Smith, who had known my parents for years, to say Mass before we spent our last moments with Mom. The seven of us, our six spouses, and Mom's in-town siblings were present; Aunt Mary and Uncle Dave had already returned to Indiana. Mass was to begin at 3:00 P.M., but for one reason or another it didn't start until about thirty minutes later. The delay was in our mother's favor. After Mass was said and my siblings and I walked to the elevator with our aunts and uncles, the elevator door opened and there was Archbishop Flynn. He had come to give Mom a final blessing.

Thus the final hour of our mother's life began with the sacrament of the Anointing of the Sick. Though Archbishop Flynn anointed Mom, it felt as if this sacred ritual helped heal all of us. He became an instrument of God's love toward Mom and everyone in the room. Bending his head, he prayed just loud enough for us to hear him: "Come, Lord Jesus. Come, Lord Jesus. Come, Lord Jesus." He repeated this phrase for several minutes, quietly but with great intensity. I had no doubt God was there, leading Mom by the hand. The room filled with love and peace, as if Mom's spiritual friends, her beloved saints and angels, all had joined with Dad to bring her home.

The archbishop left and we stepped out of the room as the machines that had kept our mother alive were silenced. John and Paul were the first ones back into Mom's room. They wanted to give her *viaticum*, a last Communion with Jesus. John's daughter Morgan had made her First Communion the previous weekend and John had saved a tiny portion of the host. It was important to him that Mom's last Communion would be made with the host from Morgan's First Communion. John stood across Mom's bed from Paul, and said, "Mom, this is for all the sacraments you will be missing with your thirty-four grandchildren." Paul then held up the host and said, "Mom, this is the body of Christ," and then responded for her with "Amen." He put it under her tongue. What a gift for Mom, John, and Morgan—three generations of our family—a true sense of what *communion* is all about. In giving her this last sacrament, Paul also received a gift. "She cried a tear," he said, "and John and I looked at each other. I like to think it was a gift of recognizing that she would soon meet Him whom she was last fed with—He who fed and sustained her for so many years."

So as with Dad, our final moments with Mom were filled with prayer and religious ritual, giving us time to say good-bye in a way she would have loved: surrounded by her family telling her how much we loved her, thanking her, and telling her it was OK for her to go. As I had wished for Dad, I hoped she would hear us as she took her last breath. And at that final moment, we saw something that made us believe she did hear us. At the moment of her death, a single tear rolled down her cheek.

Chapter Sixteen

SIGNS AS THIN PLACES

Rejoice and trust in God, for he has
given you signs that you can very well
do so, and in fact you must do so.

—ST. JOHN OF THE CROSS

MAY 3, 2002

Two days after Mom died, in the midst of our grief, we were given a lovely thin-place gift that comforted us and gave us hope, the first of several after-death signs we would receive. That Friday, Peter was going through hundreds of family photos, choosing ones to display at Mom's wake. While doing this, he found a gray envelope, addressed in her handwriting to Dad at her parents' home in Mendota Heights, Minnesota. The letter's postmark was Phoenix, Arizona, May 3, 1959— forty-five years earlier, to the day. Dad had been transferred back to Minnesota; Mom was selling their home (with the help of St. Joseph, she would insist) and we were moving to follow him.

In the envelope was a birthday card. On the cover was a fifties housewife, complete with frilly apron, sitting on a cigar-toting man's lap. It read,

"Happy Birthday, Mr. Wonderful," and opened to reveal the words, "With love from Mrs. Lucky." Beneath the words, Mom had written a message to Dad: *Happy Birthday, sweetheart! I hope this is the last of your birthdays that we will ever spend apart. All my love, Terry.* For the rest of their marriage, our parents never did spend another of his birthdays apart.

Mom's wake was May 5—what would have been Dad's seventy-fifth birthday. Was it just coincidence that Peter found this particular card exactly forty-five years after it was sent? That it celebrated Dad's birthday, which was also the day of her wake? That it proclaimed they would never again be separated on his birthday? How did the card survive the fire that had destroyed so many of our possessions? All I know is that finding it reassured us that our parents are together, never again to be apart.

On the morning of the wake, Mom's sister—our Aunt Frannie—had invited us to brunch with the rest of Mom's siblings. On the way to her home, where she and the others would tell us stories of Mom as a child, I noticed ominous clouds that indicated thunderstorms. *If Mom were here,* I thought, *she would call Aunt Kathleen to put out the statue of the Sacred Heart of Jesus.* This was another of Mom's favorite saint rituals. She would call her sister Kathleen before any outdoor family event, convinced that "putting out the statue" would prevent bad weather. We called it the "Sacred Heart statue" because it showed Christ's heart on the front of his chest. The statue had been in Mom's family for years. Gram believed it prevented rain, so before each of her children's weddings at the family home, everyone would pray for good weather, then Gram would set the statue in the direction of the ceremony. It never rained.

Mom continued this tradition. I thought this was one of her more peculiar prayer practices, and told her so in my younger, know-it-all days. "Surely you don't *really* believe that God expects people to put statues outside if they want a sunny day! Don't you think there are far more important issues for God to worry about than the weather?"

Exasperated with my disbelief, she would say, "I don't know how it works, Mary, but it does. We never had a rainy day for our outdoor weddings or family picnics. It was always a beautiful sunny day."

It was futile to argue with her. Her belief in the power of prayer and her ability to trust they would be answered had been proved to her too many times, and for her "putting out the statue" was just another ritual in which God shows he cares about our day-to-day lives, maybe even enough to send us a "weather sign." One time, Mom was in charge of planning a large family picnic. More than one hundred people were bringing potluck foods to share. The morning of the picnic, the sky was dark, cloudy, and full of rain. "It doesn't look good, Mom," I said. "Do you have a plan B?"

"Nope, it'll clear up. I just called Aunt Kathleen and told her to put the statue outside and face it north toward us." As it rained all morning, relatives called to see if the picnic was still on. To each person, Mom said, "The weather will clear up. Just come." Twenty minutes before the picnic was scheduled to begin, the rain stopped, the clouds disappeared, and the sun shone for the next five hours. Midway through the picnic, I marveled at the cloud-free sky. Just as everyone was leaving, the rain resumed. The next day, Mom called her sister and asked what time she brought the statue inside. She said 9:00 P.M.—Eastern Standard Time in Indiana, where Aunt Kathleen lived, 8:00 P.M. in Minnesota.

I still think the statue ritual is an odd way for God to demonstrate divine benevolence. But it's no different, really, than any of the signs God sends to remind us that prayer really works. When our family prayed around Mom's bedside and saw a temporary improvement in her condition, for instance, it was like the rain stopping for a while. Both events were thin-place moments that affirmed our belief in a power greater than ourselves.

At brunch on the morning of Mom's wake, Aunt Kathleen surprised us by bringing the Sacred Heart statue. "I thought this should go to your family now," she said. "I know how much the statue meant to your mother." The statue was two feet high, with Christ's arms extended to each side. His hands were gone. "Oh, they've been missing for years," Kathleen said when someone asked about them. "But we're not supposed to replace them. I was told that when the hands fall off, it means we're to be Christ's hands to others."

My sister Molly inherited the statue. And whenever there's an outdoor family event, we ask her to put it outside and face it in the direction of our gathering.

The atmosphere at Mom's wake was different than Dad's. At his wake, we all felt an almost celebratory feeling of profound gratitude that he had received what he had always asked for: the grace of a happy death. We felt numb at Mom's wake, stunned at losing her so soon after Dad. People seemed at a loss for words in expressing their sympathy. But as we left the mortuary that evening, another sign helped alleviate our grief. We all walked out at about the same time, many carrying flowers that people had sent to the funeral home. Suddenly, one of the grandchildren looked into the sky and excitedly pointed to a gorgeous rainbow. As we admired it, we noticed a second, fainter rainbow, just above the brighter one. Someone exclaimed, "It's a sign from Mom!" Just then, a flash of lightning appeared in the center of the brighter rainbow, something I'd never seen before. Looking up at the burst of light, one of the grandchildren shouted, "It's Grandpa!" It would be just like Dad to let us know, in dramatic fashion, that he was there too.

Rainbows, I have since learned, are one of the most common signs that follow the death of a loved one. Rainbows let us know that the person who died is happy and with God, yet still with us in spirit. The rainbow as a hope-inducing sign has its roots in Scripture. In the book of Genesis, after the story of the flood, God tells Noah that he will establish a covenant with him:

> *This is the sign that I am giving for all ages to come of the covenant between me and you and every living creature with you: I set my bow in the clouds to serve as a sign of the covenant between me and the earth. When I bring clouds over the earth, and the bow appears in the clouds, I will recall the covenant between me and you and all living beings, so that the waters shall never again become a flood to destroy all living beings—all mortal creatures that are on earth.... This is the sign of the covenant I have established between me and all mortal creatures that are on earth. (Genesis 19:12-17)*

This was the first time twin rainbows comforted our grieving family. It would not be the last.

MONDAY, MAY 6

As they had done for Dad's funeral, friends generously provided a charter tour bus that transported all fifty-three members of our family from the mortuary to the church, to the cemetery, and then to another church social hall where lunch was served. This kind gesture allowed us to share stories about Mom during the journey, including a thin-place experience Sheila had had the night before.

My sister and her family were staying at our parents' home. Just before leaving for the mortuary on Sunday afternoon, she packed away a quilt she had made for Mom's seventieth birthday. When designing that quilt, Sheila had sent each sibling, in-law, and grandchild a twelve-inch square of fabric to decorate with a story, poem, or other artistic creation that would be meaningful to Mom. Sheila sewed them together and the result was a poignant patchwork of colorful times spent with our mother. We gave the gift to her at her birthday party, celebrated at a resort in northern Minnesota. As her children and grandchildren unfolded the quilt off the balcony of one of our rented townhouses, Mom's eyes filled with tears. Since that day, she had proudly displayed the quilt, one of her most prized possessions, on a wall in her dining room.

After Mom died, we all agreed Sheila should have the quilt. The night of the wake, Sheila awoke shortly after midnight. After a restless hour, she took the quilt out of her suitcase, wrapped it around herself, and snuggled back into Mom and Dad's king-size bed. Like an infant held in a mother's loving arms, Sheila felt comforted and fell asleep. It was as if she could feel Mom's love embracing her, reassuring her that all would be well.

After sharing her story, Sheila reminded us of the significance of the rainbows after Mom's wake. "It was no accident that we all just happened to be coming out of the funeral home at exactly the moment the rainbows appeared," she said. Our entire family had the same interpretation, even those who might have scoffed earlier at the idea: the rainbow was a sign from Mom and Dad. Like so many others who have lost loved ones, we needed to know that our parents were still with us. Sheila encouraged the grandchildren to continue to look for signs, like the twin rainbows, that would bring continuing reassurance that Gram and Gramp were happy in their new heavenly home.

Her words proved to be prophetic almost immediately. The day after Mom's funeral, as Sheila's family turned into the driveway of their home, Ben, their youngest, pointed excitedly to the sky. Arched directly over their house, in full glory, was a gorgeous rainbow.

I first became aware of the significance of signs in the winter of 1994. The signs began as an intuitive sense that something was wrong with a friend named Tom who was my boss and mentor from a job I held a few years before. Tom and I had kept in sporadic contact, speaking by phone or having lunch a few times, but I had not seen him in two years. When I didn't respond to the vague but persistent feeling, a voice in my head became specific: "Tom is very ill. Call him." This inner directive nagged at me until I called a former colleague, who told me she had just visited with Tom and learned he was seriously ill. She thought it was cancer.

I couldn't sleep that night. I lay awake, feeling guilty for ignoring the inner voice, yet rationalizing that he didn't need to be bothered by a coworker from his past. But I wondered: *Was there something I was supposed to do? Some role I was supposed to play?* Had Tom been a close friend or someone I saw frequently, I would have known what to do. I didn't know his family; I had met his wife just once, at a Christmas party years earlier. I didn't want to intrude if indeed he was very sick. Self-doubt prompted me to do what I often do when I'm unsure how to respond to a predicament: I prayed. And I asked for a sign to guide me.

Seconds later, I squinted at the clock. It was 3:00 A.M. I got up and decided to clean out a small kitchen closet that was a mess. While sifting through mounds of paper and miscellaneous clutter, I came across a page that had been torn out of *Family Circle*. A quick glance revealed no reason to save it; it contained no interesting recipes, no diet that promised to shave ten pounds off in a week. Then, in a box of type on the upper left of the page, I saw a brief article about a woman who was diagnosed with CML—chronic myelogenous leukemia. The woman told how she attributed her recovery to good medical care, a successful bone marrow transplant, and family and friends who prayed for her, sent her encouraging notes, and engulfed her in love and kindness. I interpreted the coincidence of finding the article to mean that I should call Tom and offer my friendship.

When I did so the next day, I uncovered another coincidence: Tom had CML. Like the woman in the article, he had the treatment option of a bone marrow transplant. When I asked if there was anything I could do, he responded simply, "Yes. Pray for me." Before we hung up, we agreed to get together after I returned from a retreat the following week. At the retreat, I prayed for a cure for Tom, as well as for continued guidance concerning how I might help him.

Over the next few months, I experienced several other coincidences and intuitive promptings. For example, I happened to run into Tom at the Mall of America shopping center the day after our phone call. "Isn't this interesting?" he said. "After not seeing you for two years, I talk to you twice in two days." I wondered if this coincidence was telling me something. *Maybe it was simply to remind me to stay in touch with Tom,* I thought.

Because he had asked for prayers, I prayed for Tom daily. We had several conversations before he died in November 1994. Reflecting on the final months of his life, I realized that my reaction to his situation had been influenced by things that seemed to have happened for a reason. When I was unsure what I should do to help him, I asked God for clarity. And what I received were signs that guided me.

In later conversations with Tom's wife, Joan (who has since become a good friend), I learned that, like Dad, Tom was surrounded by people who helped him cope with his illness and eventual death. Each person, it seemed, had a role to play. His family and close friends were with him constantly, showering him with love; his extended family created a mailing list that solicited prayers and support from a wider circle of friends. One of his best friends even shaved his head in a show of solidarity with Tom, who had lost his hair during chemo. Tom laughed when his newly bald friend visited him in the hospital.

Eventually, I realized that my role in Tom's situation was small yet significant. From our conversations, I learned how important his faith had been in dealing with his illness. When he needed to decide if he should go ahead with the risky bone marrow transplant, I suggested he go to the retreat center my father and husband often attended. He did, and later said it was one of the best things he could have done. With his characteristic optimism, he even made plans to visit a retreat center in Arizona the following year. Before he entered the hospital a few months later for the transplant, Tom told me he was hopeful it would be successful. But he also accepted the possibility that it would fail. "I am ready," he told me, "for whatever happens."

At the time, I was amazed how peaceful he was. At first, the transplant did seem to work; Tom survived the crucial first twenty-one days. But then he got an infection, which his immune system was too weak to fight, and he was in a coma for several days. He died surrounded by his family and the music of the song he loved, "Amazing Grace." Joan later shared that their family noted several little signs that reassured them that Tom's spirit was at peace, yet still with them.

Tom's death marked the beginning of a period of spiritual growth for me, for two reasons: First, by paying attention to the thin-place experiences when God was whispering in my ear or nudging me, I developed a more personal relationship with God. No longer was God an abstraction that I prayed to but never really knew. My prayers were heard and answered in a way that became a dialogue of sorts: I asked, then waited for a response. And responses came frequently: as an intuitive or direct inner voice, or as something someone said at just the right time, or as a coincidence that provided help or guidance. With each thin-place experience, I felt closer to God; each time was a validation that God knows each of us intimately and "calls us by name." Even when it seemed God was not answering my prayers, I learned to let go because I could trust that God knew better than me what I really needed. My faith increased tremendously.

Second, nearly every time someone else tells me about a thin-place experience, it becomes one for me. In the years since Tom's death, I have heard hundreds of accounts of incidents that seemed to happen for a reason. The stories first came from family and friends, then later from people who came to me for spiritual direction. Many of the stories told of comforting incidents that occurred after a person's loved one had died. Often, in the midst of telling his or her story, the person would lean over as if sharing a deep secret and say something like, "I don't tell many people about this." I started asking people why they were so reluctant to share their spiritual experiences—for that is often what a sign becomes for them—when they interpret it as a tangible manifestation of God's action in their lives. Here's what some of them said:

> *"Others will think it was too weird."*

> *"No one will believe it really happened or agree that it was a sign."*

> *"I don't want to appear as if I have some sort of pipeline to God. I'm no more special than anyone else, so why should something like this happen to me?"*

> *"God can't/won't do something like this."*

> *"My minister/priest/other clergy would say (or said) this sign is not from God but from the devil." (One woman told me her minister said this about a comforting vision in which she saw her deceased mother. The man's condemnation about something that helped bring peace in the midst of grief so upset the woman that she not only refused to return to her church, she changed religions, and is much happier.)*

Each statement seemed filled with fear or judgment, and echoed some of my own reasons for not talking about spiritual experiences. I too am afraid of being judged by others. I too judge myself as being unworthy. This fear, if we give in to it, can be destructive in two ways. First, it causes us to discount the validity of our own spiritual experiences and rob us of their meaning. Second, the fear of being judged by others often causes us to resist sharing our stories of signs and other spiritual experiences. Thus, we are deprived of the opportunity to enhance not only our own faith but the faith of others. We also are denied the opportunity to develop the soul friendships that so often result from sharing our spiritual stories. I began asking myself, *Who am I to decide what God can and cannot do?*

If only we could remember that God is always available to help us deal with fear. Scholars claim the most repeated phrase in the Bible is some variation of the words, "Do not be afraid." In the Spring 2003 issue of "Loyola Letter," Joanne Dehmar, a spiritual director at Loyola Spiritual Renewal Resource, in St. Paul, wrote, "Perhaps God in all wisdom knew we needed to be reassured that we need not live in fear. What follows 'Do not be afraid' are the words 'I am with you.'"

In addition to paying attention to my own experiences, I have learned from others that examples of signs include hearing the "still, small voice within" or just knowing something with a confidence that is unshakable. Often people notice something in nature, like a rainbow, that provides comfort immediately after someone dies. God's comforting presence can be conveyed through other people, inner voices/intuitive promptings, or things (like coincidences) that seem to happen for a reason, as if meant to be.

It's helpful to share our observations and interpretations of signs. Telling others about our spiritual experiences in a nonjudgmental environment is an opportunity to share faith, discern meaning, and validate our insights with each other and to develop soul friendships.

Signs occur regardless of one's spiritual/religious beliefs and backgrounds. If we listen to the stories of others, without discounting ones from people who do not share our own beliefs, we will learn much about the many ways God is active in all peoples' lives.

Signs often require discernment, to determine if they really are from God or will help us decide where God is leading us. I pray for guidance about signs and ask: Is this experience consistent with the words of sacred scripture and with the actions of a loving God? What are the fruits/potential fruits of the experience? Did I feel peaceful or comforted by the experience?

Once we start noticing signs and responding to them, they seem to appear regularly. This is also true of synchronicity, the meaningful coincidences that seem too significant to be considered just a fluke or fate. Julia Cameron's excellent book, *The Artist's Way*, encourages readers to watch for synchronicity as part of enhancing creativity as well as fostering spiritual growth. The more people notice them, the more they do seem to occur.

In the United States, studies show that nearly 97 percent of us believe in some sort of higher power. A few years ago, I read somewhere that research showed that of that figure, approximately 25 percent of us have a hard time conceiving of a truly personal God, one who cares about each of us and is actually involved in our daily lives. Hearing about and experiencing signs can affirm our hope that God not only exists but is constantly communicating with us. Whether we notice and respond to those communications is up to us. Signs also enable us to live life more fully, to grow in wisdom. They encourage us to love each other, to love ourselves, and to love God. The realization of how much God loves each of us, enough to become involved on a personal level in our lives, can transform our world and give us an intimation of the love we will experience in the next world.

Coincidences can be a wonderful tool in helping us create a discernment process, to help guide our lives. I now pay close attention to things that seem to happen for a reason, including people, inner voices or intuitive messages, or observable, external things, like coincidences and other serendipitous events. Someone once said that when something happens three times, it is like God is telling us what to do. Scripture is filled with events that happened three times. And three is the number the ancient Celts and other cultures felt signaled the presence of the Divine. I now pay special attention when a similar event happens three times, and I consider whether God is communicating a message or suggesting a specific action.

For example, I have been a hospice volunteer. That decision was motivated by three events that occurred within two days. First, a notice appeared in our parish bulletin, describing an upcoming training session and recruiting hospice volunteers. After reading the notice, I thought this might be something I would like to do someday—but not right then.

Second, the day after the notice, Beth and I were serving meals at the Dorothy Day Center in St. Paul. As we set the tables for dinner, she mentioned an article she had saved for me from the newsletter published by the hospital where she worked. It was about a nurse who was a hospice volunteer. "I think you should do this too," Beth told me.

Finally, later that same evening, an older gentleman who was also serving meals said how he often visited the sick and dying as a volunteer with his church. "You should do this too, Mary," he said, repeating Beth's words. "You would be good at it and you would love the work."

I resisted the idea of becoming a hospice volunteer. My life was already chaotic enough. A part-time job, other volunteer commitments, and my four children, ages eleven to eighteen, kept me plenty busy. But because I believe God sometimes communicates to us through incidents that happen in threes, I decided to go through the training. To make a long story short, my first patient was Susan, the woman I mentioned earlier. My relationship with her eventually motivated me to change careers. During the seven-month relationship that preceded her death, we had several spiritual discussions about dying, faith, and prayer. She often called me her "spiritual director," even though she knew I lacked any formal training. At the time, I was a marketing manager for a creativity consulting firm that helped companies generate ideas for strategies and new products— not exactly a spiritually oriented profession (although there is a strong connection between creativity and spirituality, as observed by Julia Cameron).

Also during this time, my own spiritual director suggested I consider taking the discernment class she was teaching in the summer. Another coincidence. Despite misgivings about adding yet another activity to my already full schedule, I took that class and loved it. I ended up quitting a fairly lucrative career at the worst possible time, with four children either in or headed for college. Therefore, my eventual career as a spiritual director (and later, as executive director of a nonprofit holistic healing center) was the result of a decision made to respond to something that happened three times. And to trust in the wisdom of that decision, without knowing where it would lead.

Paying attention to signs—coincidences, intuitive promptings, and other "things" that seem to happen for a reason—affirms to me that the world is an amazing thin place. This attentiveness to divine providence, manifesting God's personal involvement in my life, has become perhaps the most important aspect of my own spiritual journey.

All of my sisters, and probably my brothers, know about my propensity to see incidents like finding Dad's prayer card as "signs." I believe synchronicity, an especially meaningful coincidence, signals the presence of God in our lives. Over the past few years, many things in my life had occurred so serendipitously that they seemed divinely orchestrated. When they've occurred as a series of events that provide more insight than is possible to imagine on our own, it's been hard *not* to conclude that they are divinely inspired. The incidents were "meant to be," the phrase used by many people who have told me about their similar experiences. Being on the lookout for signs and discovering their meaning is a rich opportunity for living in a thin-place world. I now notice signs all the time. Paying attention to these signs with discernment can transform a person's life.

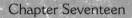

Chapter Seventeen

After-Death Thin Places

Death is not putting out the light.
It is only extinguishing a lamp because
the day has come.

—Rabindranath Tagore

June 2002

Beth and I each had heard stories about thin-place incidents that occurred after people died. Some of hers were from the families of patients she had been particularly close to before they died. Many of mine were from my spiritual directees, as well as from friends and acquaintances. Beth and I shared some of the especially poignant stories and agreed that hearing them lessened our own fear of death.

The grief of losing two parents so abruptly manifested itself in many ways: forgetfulness, even more than normal; spaciness; tears at the slightest provocation—for example, hearing a song from our childhood or one of Dad's favorites. Seeing the promotions for Mother's Day less than two weeks after Mom's death was more difficult than I could have imagined. Several times, I walked out of stores in tears.

The kindness of friends and family helped, but what consoled us most were the thin-place experiences we continued to have—and still have—after our parents died. Rainbows were just one example of incidents that brought comfort and reassurance and hope.

Some people have suggested that those who notice signs and other thin-place experiences do so because they are always looking for them. My teenage children, for example, tease me for "seeing the hand of God in almost everything." Others claim signs are the result of our imagination. I believe God communicates with us in many ways, including through our imagination, as well as through dreams, intuition, coincidences, and nature. Within our family, the incidents began soon after Mom's death, and, consistent with the "coincidences are God's way of remaining anonymous" theory, they often occurred on birthdays and other days that held special significance.

Several of us noticed signs on our first Father's Day without Dad, almost all with a common theme: hearing songs we associated with him. In previous years, most of us in-towners would have gathered at our parents' home on Father's Day, with each family bringing a pot-luck dish to complete a barbecued meal served on the back deck. This year, Paul joined me and my family for Mass, followed by brunch at one of our favorite breakfast hangouts. Just before Mass began, Paul leaned over to me and whispered, "I wonder if we will get any song signs from Dad today." Minutes later, we opened our songbooks to see the lyrics of "On Eagles' Wings" and both of us laughed. Dad didn't care for the song, but he knew Mom loved it. "I guess Dad's throwing a bone to Mom on this one," Paul said with a smile.

Hundreds of miles apart, Dennis and Emmy also heard "On Eagles' Wings" in church that first Father's Day. After Mass, Dennis's wife, Julie, said she had asked for a sign, specifically to bring them comfort at Mass. And John had his own song sign: At his daughter Molly's recital on Father's Day, "Down to the River to Pray" was sung as part of a medley of songs from O Brother, Where Art Thou?

When I checked my voicemail later that day, I heard the familiar recording that accompanies messages that have been saved for a long time: "You have had the following message for 100 days, the maximum time allowed." I held my breath, wondering if I would hear one of my parents' voices, having saved and resaved messages I'd received from both of them. It was Mom. My eyes became teary as I listened to her voice, to the simple message conveyed by breathless words punctuated with coughs, indicating the severity of her lung disease. She had left the message after I had called to check on her, just a week or so before she entered the hospital. She rattled off a chatty list of things she had done that day, reflecting her refusal to let her illness or grief slow her down:

> *I'm just checking in to let you know I'm fine and dandy. I was just in town and went to Mass at St. Joe's this morning at nine, then I had a cup of coffee with Maureen, stopped by Emmy's and went to the post office, the bank, and all that busy work ... and it's two o'clock and I'm home safe and sound. Talk to you later.*

Once again, the timing was significant, as both Dad and Mom seemed to be letting us know on this difficult day that they were "home safe and sound."

The next day, nine of the ten siblings gathered for what we had dubbed the "picking day"—the time for divvying up our parents' belongings. Dennis had planned to be in town that day for some other event, probably a golf tournament, so we timed "picking day" so he could be with us. Paul had e-mailed photos of every item to Sheila so she could be included via telephone from Portland.

I had been a bit nervous about this evening. So far, we had been getting along wonderfully during and following Mom's and Dad's deaths. We had never spent as much time together as adults as we did during their final days. We had handled our grief, stress, and tough decision-making with much humor, dignity, and grace. The faith of our parents had sustained us; we had prayed together more during those times than ever before. We all wanted this evening to go well, so we agreed in advance not to declare preferences for certain items to prevent hard feelings if several people wanted the same thing. We had also agreed on a process that seemed fair: We would return gifts made to Mom and Dad to the person who had given them. We'd then view the items and divide them via a lottery system recommended by friends who had been through this process. Whatever was left over would be sold at an estate sale or given to charity.

Walking through the house was surreal but cathartic, as we remembered the history of this platter or that table. I felt strangely detached from this process; I was surprised at how little their stuff meant to me. After the tour, we poured glasses of wine in the living room and toasted each other in thanksgiving for the closeness we shared during the past few months. Our lottery system was simple and fair: Each person chose a number between one and ten. Whoever picked "one" went first, followed by those with numbers two through ten. Then the order was reversed, from ten to one, so that the first person didn't choose for another nineteen picks.

We started with the more sentimental items. Coincidentally, everyone seemed to get his or her first or second choice. I had picked the number nine and still got something I hoped I would: a silver bracelet that likely belonged to our Grandmother Gongie. After this first round of picking, we walked around the house a second time to review the more functional items remaining. After declaring our preferences, Dennis wrote down a number and whoever guessed the number closest to it got the item. Within a few pleasant hours, we packed up what we could to take home. Large furniture would be moved later.

I left around 1:00 A.M. with two medium-sized boxes filled with the few things I wanted. Dad's post-fire prediction that "there won't be much for you all to fight over when we're gone" proved true, and when I got home, I received a timely reminder of his wisdom. Despite the late hour, I was too buzzed up from the evening's activities, so I checked our phone messages and heard one of my many saved messages from my parents. This message was from Dad, one he had left late the previous year. As I listened, I cried and laughed at the same time:

> Mary, do you realize since 1969 that we've had either a trailer or motor home in our yard—or some sort of recreational vehicle? So today was the end of an era, bittersweet. We sold the motor home! And, it's kinda sad, Mary [fake crying], so I thought I'd talk to my "spiritual director" about it [he and Mom laugh]. Anyway, the money is in the bank and we delivered the thing today. Didn't get what we wanted, but as your mother says, "It's only money." That's what her father

told her. Ha! Ha! Anyway [responding to my invitation to take them to lunch], yes, we will have lunch. We'll be going to the doctor a lot after the first of the year, so I got your nice note and thank you. And we'll do lunch—we'll be available for lunch lots of times when Mother starts her three-day-a week treatment [shots for her IPF disease]. Hope everything is OK. Good-bye.

Of all the days to receive a thin-place message! What a blessing it was to hear Dad's voice, reminding me of the insignificance of material things—a message that reaffirmed one of their key philosophies of life: that "it's only stuff," that heavenly rewards outweigh earthly possessions.

Chapter Eighteen

SHARING THIN-PLACE STORIES

So what is it that helps you pay attention? Some people walk or read scripture or sing a hymn. Some do a simple
review of noticing what they are
grateful for. Pretty soon the gifts we
notice become traceable to the Giver
and prayer happens. I find that I am
helped in sharing my stories with others. People help affirm my observations that it is God I have stumbled
on, or question my perception. I hear
another's story, and... I am able to
recognize God in new ways.

—REVEREND JOHN ACKERMAN

JUNE 2002

One of my favorite topics as a speaker is
the healing power of friendships. At the
holistic healing center where I work, we
offer support groups for seriously ill people to
express their feelings and share their stories.
Research shows that this type of social support
strengthens immune systems and fosters healing.
Sharing one's story with a close friend can be a

similar healing opportunity; when such conversations involve a spiritual dimension, a soul friendship can develop. To have a soul friend truly is a blessing. Soul friends talk with each other about their spiritual beliefs and their thin-place stories without fear of judgment. Sharing such stories deepens our relationship with each other as well as with God, and helps us to discover their divine nature, clarify their meaning, and discern if and how we should respond.

The love that exists between soul friends, as in other affectionate relationships, is a love that never dies. A few years ago, my good friend Holly shared with me a story that demonstrated the everlasting nature of soul friendship. It involved her husband's grandmother, Cecelia ("Cece"), and Cece's friend, Agnes.

The friendship began when Agnes's son married Cece's daughter. As their children became parents and then grandparents, the friendship between Agnes and Cece deepened. Despite their age difference (Cece was nearly ten years older than Agnes), they enjoyed many years of each other's company. As Cece approached her mid-eighties, her mind became more and more confused, and her family eventually made the difficult decision to move her to a nursing home. A true friend, Agnes visited Cece almost daily, even after Cece could no longer recognize her.

When Agnes was in her late eighties, she often wondered aloud why Cece continued to live long past her prime. Agnes's wit was as sharp as her mind: "God must have forgotten my friend Cece," she would say to nurses, family, and friends—anyone who would listen. "If I go first, I will tell Him to go get her and bring her straight to heaven!" Everyone laughed, never dreaming that Agnes, the picture of health, would go first. But Agnes did die first, one Sunday morning, without warning. Just as her son's family prepared to leave their home for her funeral Mass, they received a call from their other grandmother's nursing home: Cece had just passed away. "As news of Cece's death spread through the church during Agnes's funeral, people starting smiling and some even laughed," my friend Holly later recalled. "Those who knew the two women well and had heard Agnes's promise to talk to God if she got to heaven first loved the idea that the two buddies were together again."

I had told some of my siblings the Cece and Agnes story when it occurred. I also shared the story with others after Mom died, because it is so filled with hope in its reaffirmation of everlasting friendship and love.

The story also sheds light on something I have wondered about: Just what is the nature of our soul, the part of us that lives on? Does it have a personality, similar to the one we have on earth? Many times, the thin-place stories I hear cause me to believe that our soul, the essence of who we are, retains aspects of our personality on earth. Perhaps this is how we "just know" when our deceased loved ones are present; we sense their unmistakable personalities. Agnes's sense of humor seemed reaffirmed in the timing of her death. It was as if she and God really did have a chat about bringing Cece to heaven after Agnes died so the friends could be reunited straight-away. The thought of it brought smiles even in the midst of grief.

After our parents died, my family had many thin-place experiences that reminded us of Mom's and Dad's personalities. We e-mailed our stories back and forth, grateful to affirm these special connections to our parents, but also to each other through our faith. I have become more comfortable sharing my spiritual experiences with my own family, not just with Beth.

I sent the first e-mail. Our oldest son, Peter, knew that his grandmother always prayed when she needed help. He couldn't help wondering if Mom may have helped his prayers become answered when he lost his wallet in Chicago, where he attended college:

June 19, 2002—Peter took a city bus into Chicago and realized as soon as he got off that he left his wallet containing all of his ID cards and some cash on the bus. He was planning to fly to Oregon the following day and without any photo ID, it would be impossible for him to travel. Understandably, he was very upset.

He was desperate, near panic. Suddenly, he remembered how his grandmother always prayed for help—especially when something was lost. It was almost like he heard her voice in his head, telling him to do the same. So, despite lingering questions of faith, he prayed that he would find the wallet. He promised God that if he did find it, he would donate all the money in his wallet to the nearest church.

A half hour later, a bus stopped, where Peter was waiting anxiously. He asked the driver if he had been by earlier that day. The driver said he was by, but it was about an hour ago, so Peter didn't think it was the right bus. Despite his doubts, something compelled him to tell the driver that he lost the wallet, and he left his phone number and asked the driver to please call him if one is found. At the same time as he related his dilemma, a teenage boy got on the bus and he must have overheard Peter, who had stepped off the bus to wait for another one. Suddenly, Peter heard a shout, as the boy yelled out a window that he found the wallet, having just sat in the same seat where Peter had been seated. As the bus pulled away from the curb, the boy tossed the wallet out the window to my astonished and grateful son.

Realizing this was all a bit too serendipitous, he thanked the God whose existence he has so frequently questioned. True to his promise, he took all the money in his wallet and put it in a box for the poor at a nearby church.

Several of us had experiences on Mom's birthday, June 26, including Paul, who had stayed at our parents' house the night before to take care of a few last tasks, like cleaning Dad's boat and moving the pop-up trailer:

June 26—I woke up this morning and the first thing I did was say, "Happy birthday, Mom." As I was about to leave, I received the birthday gift. Right next to the mailbox that is a replica of Mom's childhood home, I noticed a single rose. And with Dad's digital camera, I am able to share that gift with y'all as we remember Mom on her day. Funny ... as I was preparing to move the popup, I walked very near this little flower but didn't notice it until this morning. Thanks, Mom. I'm sure this is your way of saying,"Love ya!"

Mom was named for St. Therese of Liseaux. When Mom had something especially important to pray for, she said a novena to St. Therese, also known as "the Little Flower," who, on her deathbed, promised to "send a shower of roses from heaven." After reading Paul's note, Molly told us that she too had been at our parents' house the day before to put mulch around the mailbox, yet saw nothing where Paul later found the rose. Two days later, Dennis noticed a coincidence related to Paul's "rose story" that involved Dennis's wife, Julie:

> *June 28—Julie ran across this wonderful photo that was included in my photo box. [Attached was a photo of Mom kneeling in the same spot where Paul saw the rose. She had a rose in her hand.] Another "sign" that Mom and Dad will always be with us.*

Maureen's experience on Mom's birthday was a dream. The scene was near our former parish in St. Paul, and included one of Mom's typical daily activities, going to Mass:

> *June 26—Early this morning I had my most vivid dream of Mom since her death. It was very simple and fleeting. She was in our old neighborhood ... and appeared to be walking home from Mass at Immaculate Heart of Mary Church. In the dream, I was driving and I knew she had died, so when I saw a woman that resembled her, I turned around quickly. There she was, clear as could be, in the white nylon wind suit she often wore. Then I turned to the front and she was there again, this time in a white outfit. Don't know what to make of that, other than she was surely lurking in my subconscious on her birthday. A psychologist would probably say the white had to do with purity or her new state as an angel.*

Peter's thin-place story involved his wife, Jill, their three-year-old son, Will, and one of Mom's favorite hymns:

> *June 26—Our boy Will shall be singing "Happy Birthday" all day to Mom, so if you forget, know he is*

singing for you too…. I guess this is the way holidays and special occasions will be for the rest of our lives. I am glad that Mom and Dad are finding ways to send little messages on not only these days, but in our everyday lives. They seem to find a way to do so just when we need it. For example, last week Jill and I were swinging on the porch swing, per Mom's orders, and having a heavy discussion about whether I should leave my job, what it would mean to our finances, would I find a job in this tough market, etc., when suddenly we hear a voice and it's Will, singing the responsorial psalm from Mom's funeral: "Shepherd me, O God, beyond my wants, beyond my fears, from death into life…" Neither Jill nor I had ever heard him sing that song before, and we just looked at each other in amazement. I hope that amazement continues when we receive these "messages" and that our senses are not dulled into missing them.

Later that day, Peter wrote again:

I was talking to one of the executive assistants here at work, and she was asking how things were going with our grieving. I told her that we are still getting some peace from little "signs" that Mom and Dad are still with us. She asked if I had found any pennies lately, noting that the saying "pennies from heaven" comes from the belief that whenever you find a penny it means someone in heaven loves and cares about you—and wants you to know. I got goose bumps… but not because I found a penny today. It was because this morning as I was walking through our back lawn I found there, in the middle of the grass, a dime. I explained to Cheryl that since Mom had ten kids, she loves and cares for us ALL—and wanted us to know.

The mention of the dime reminded me of Mom as well:

June 30—OK, this might be a really old memory for just us girls. Remember what Mom always said as we went out the door on dates? "*Take a dime with you in case you need to call home.*"

Molly's message on Mom's birthday involved a gift within a gift:

> *July 2—On Mom's birthday, I received a package in the mail from a woman I used to work with years ago. She had made me a charm bracelet. Each charm was something significant in Mom and Dad's life together. The middle charms were two hearts joined together to symbolize their love for each other. Other charms were a boat, a bus, and a schoolhouse, yarn with knitting needles, a rocking chair, the Bible, a storybook, and a teddy bear. Then she had an explanation for each charm. Apparently she has gotten to know Mary Galvin [our cousin], who shared with her many stories about Mom and Dad that Mary remembered. Needless to say, I was very touched by this gift. The woman had no idea it was Mom's birthday when she sent it.*

DECEMBER 2002

Our first Christmas without Mom and Dad was especially difficult. We continued the tradition of gathering at Emmy's house on Christmas Eve, trying to lose ourselves in the excitement of the younger grandchildren, but our sense of loss was too great. Toward the end of the evening, however, Emmy lifted our spirits with a thin-place story that reminded us of Mom's belief in angels.

A few days earlier, Emmy and her husband, Greg, were scrambling to get their house ready and decorated for our party. Adding to the chaos of the usual hectic preparations was that their basement was under construction. They barely got the carpeting down before Christmas, much less had decorated the tree. Emmy had taken a break to go through a box of memorabilia from our parents' home, looking for any Christmas decorations from our childhood. As she explored the various odds and ends in the box, she noticed a gallon-sized plastic bag filled with off-white crocheted items. In it she found several crocheted ornaments—a few stars and a snowflake or two, but mostly angels. Emmy recognized the angels as the ones Mom had won as part of a door prize at a charity auction several years ago. The angels had been the decorations on a tabletop tree covered with white lights. Mom had been thrilled to win the door prize, partly because she was such an angel fan and partly because she rarely won anything.

Emmy noticed that the angel ornaments were no longer bright white; they were almost beige. After thinking about it for a moment, it dawned on her: the decorations had survived the fire at our parents' home. Pulling the angels from the bag one by one, she lined them up in neat rows on the dining room table, wondering how to use them in remembrance of our parents that Christmas Eve. She decided to let each grandchild put an angel on the tree. Underneath the last browned ornament in the bag was one more angel—one Emmy had never seen before. It was brilliant white in contrast to the others. It also wasn't crocheted with yarn like the others; it was more delicate, like a lace doily. On the angel's skirt was a pink rose—another "rose sign" from Mom.

In the midst of her party preparations, Emmy's heart had been especially heavy as she was constantly reminded that this would be our first Christmas without Mom and Dad. She wanted the feeling of connection to them that signs give her, but she hadn't experienced any lately, or maybe she was just too busy to notice them. The day before discovering the angel ornaments, she had prayed and specifically asked for a sign. After finding the angel with the rose on her skirt, Emmy could feel Mom reminding her to stay calm, that everything would get done. She could almost hear Mom whispering encouragement to her, saying, "You can do it." Emmy could sense both of our parents telling her, "Don't worry or be sad. We'll still be with you this Christmas too, just as we always have. Even though you won't see us, we will be there." When Emmy shared the story of finding the special angel ornament that Christmas Eve, we all sensed that our parents were present. The ornament was yet another reminder that Mom and Dad, along with the angels, will be with us on every Christmas and whenever we miss them.

Sharing our thin-place stories has made us siblings aware of how important it is to share them with our children. Their understanding of their personal relationship with God is still growing and maturing, but they are finding their own ways of honoring and connecting with their grandparents' faith. Molly's oldest, Danny, for example, made his "senior quote" in his high-school yearbook a tribute to one of Dad's final lines: "Keep the faith and the faith will keep you." Carolyn, Kevin's oldest daughter, has felt Mom and Dad's presence through her connection to nature. She has sensed Dad talking to her "from the other side," just as he promised he would before he died. She also believes her grandmother talks to her. Knowing I was collecting family stories related to Mom and Dad's deaths, Carolyn e-mailed me several of her stories, many involving her international competitions in biathlon events. One story reveals a thin-place connection with Dad:

> *While I was able to embrace the stories and signs that others had about Grandma and Grandpa, I think that for a long time, and maybe somewhat still now, I was not very connected to my spiritual life. However, I have had some very tangible signs from them while I've been traveling.... I was in Silver Star, British Columbia, for a training camp in November. We go there every year and I've sent Grandma and Grandpa many a card from this beautiful skier's paradise. One day our morning workout was just a long easy ski, so we all headed out on our own at our own pace to enjoy the beautiful sunny day. I skied halfway up the mountain, then decided to ski down a dead-end trail that was great terrain and had a fabulous view at the end. When I reached the end of the trail, I was just elated from the warmth of the sun, fresh air, and endorphins pounding through me. To top it off, in front of me was a beautiful, tree-lined valley with wisps of clouds floating about. I stopped to take it in and decided to tell God he had done a fine job making this corner of the world.*
>
> *As I stood there, many little birds made me think of Grandpa and the bird feeder on the deck, and I said "Hello" to him. As I was skiing back up on the trail, one of the little clouds from the valley rose through the trees and engulfed me. It's a great feeling to be engulfed*

in a cloud, but I was still thinking of Grandpa when this happened, so this cloud seemed like one of the big, engulfing hugs he would always give me as I leaned over his easy chair that sat facing the birds on the deck.

Another of Carolyn's stories involved Mom:

Again in Silver Star, I suddenly woke up one night because there was a very wet and cold tear running down my cheek. It was such a big tear that it woke me up and I could feel it slowly meandering down my face. I got up, went to the bathroom, and drank some water. Then, when I lay down again, still confused about why I had been tearing, I remembered Grandma and her last tear. Then I remembered that Grandma would always get up and walk at night [because of her restless legs], and a conversation I had with her came back to me. Once I was talking to Grandma about praying because I was frustrated when I would fall asleep before finishing my prayers. She told me she did that too, but whenever she didn't finish her rosary, she would wake up and finish it. If she fell asleep again, something else would wake her up and she'd continue it again. I knew that this tear was a reminder from Grandma to say my prayers. It was also a sign that she is up there with my guardian angel, keeping an eye on me.

When Carolyn was having problems adjusting to teammates, another "Mom connection" came to her:

We all have our "moments," and when you're on a team with people, you're forced to see more of their moments than you normally would because we travel with each other so much. I was letting some of my teammates' moments get to me in Austria in December, so I decided to go on a walk to the village church for a little huddle. I knelt down in the beautiful, ornate church and immediately started rattling off prayers. Then I thought maybe I should let someone else do the talking. So, I sat back and looked around at all the art and asked God, "Are you really here, in this cold, overdecorated building?"

And as soon as I had finished the question, a voice in my head answered right back, "Of course, He's here—He's everywhere, all the time. And He's in EVERYONE all the time." It was immediately comforting to be reminded that God is in my teammates, even at their low moments, and this made it easier to like them all the time. It's been a much nicer winter since then.

I know this reminder came from Grandma. It was a "Grandma answer," loud and clear. I miss them terribly, and it makes me so sad to think of how sick they were, but in a way, it is easier to talk to them right now. They are always there, anywhere in the world, any time zone or hour of the night. Also, now they can be with me on all my trips and instead of seeing postcards. They can see everything I see!"

In my case, sharing thin-place stories with my children has allowed me to share an important aspect of my spirituality: the unwavering belief that God is active, on a personal level, in our day-to-day lives. My sons and daughter aren't always comfortable with "God-talk," but on those rare occasions when they are, and they share their inexplicable experiences, our conversations often include a spiritual dimension, without even mentioning the word "God." In the fall of 2002, for instance, our son Bill sent us the following e-mail from Galway, where he was attending Ireland's National University for a semester. His thin-place experience was connected to one of Dad's favorite places, a small village on the west coast of Ireland called Doolin:

September 17—This weekend we went to the Cliffs of Mohrer, which were spectacular. Luckily, we went on one of the most beautiful days of the year, and we are going to have some great pictures. Joe, Mitch, and I spent the night in the small Irish town of Doolin … the "music capital of Ireland." We sat in a pub surrounded by sixty-year-old Irish people and listened as they sang *beautiful Irish songs all night long. It was really a great experience."*

I wrote back:

September 17—Just had to tell you that Doolin is the town my father wrote about on the bottom of a picture I found. In case you hadn't heard that story, here it is:

A few weeks ago, we were going through a few more photos from our parents' house and Emmy said to be sure to go through Mom's scrapbook of Ireland. In there, we found a picture of my mom in front of a framed map of "the Burren," which you probably know is the inland area south of Galway Bay and east of the Cliffs of Mohrer. In the photo, my mother is pointing to the town of Balleyvaughn, which you must have driven through. The interesting thing is that out of all the hundreds of towns in Ireland, that particular town is where I would have been on May 1, the day she died. Since we knew she was dying, I had to cancel a tour [with Irish author, theologian John O'Donohue] that was to have started that day, and Balleyvaughn is the town we would have stayed in for my time in Ireland. What a coincidence.

And on the bottom of the photo was a rare note from my father, and your comments about the music now help me understand what he said. He wrote, "From Doolin (music) to Balleyvaughn, a beautiful coastal drive en route to Galway." I didn't understand why he wrote "music," but now I do. A few days after I found this photo, your father asked me what I wanted for my fiftieth birthday, and that's when I told him I wanted our family to go to Ireland. To visit you, of course, and be-cause my father told us just before he died to go there as often as we could, because "there is nothing like treading on the ground where your ancestors once walked."

So you, dear son, have been "treading on the ground" where not only your ancestors from hundreds of years ago once walked, but where your grandfather more recently "once walked"—because if there was good music in Doolin, you can be assured that Grandpa Treacy was in those pubs, enjoying them as much as you did. And if you were in those pubs this weekend, you were there on their fifty-first wedding anniversary, which was Sunday, September 15. How perfectly appropriate is this timing? Just a year ago, we were dancing and enjoying Irish music during that wonderful fiftieth wedding anniversary party, and now you are actually in Ireland this year, listening to Irish music on their anniversary. I hope you felt their "presence" with you, because I suspect both of them were with you in spirit.

As you walk and golf and enjoy the land "where your ancestors once walked," be attentive to the feeling that those ancestors, including my parents, will walk with you in spirit. There is a concept in Celtic spirituality called "thin places," places in Ireland and other parts of the world where the veil between this world and the next one is very thin. And you can "feel" the spirits/angels/ God with you there.

I could feel it in the hospice where my father died, as soon as I walked in the door. Lest you think this is all a bit wacky, know that it is consistent with what Irish people have believed for centuries. That heritage, tradition, and genetic make-up is yours too. So watch for any connections, especially to Grandpa Treacy. It's real.

Bill's reply:

September 18—It is amazing that I was in Doolin on your parents' anniversary, listening to real Irish music. It is no surprise at all that Grandpa loved Doolin. The music was wonderful, and I know Gramp would have had a great time in the pub we were in. In fact, when I look back on it, many of the people in that pub were much like Grandpa: jovial, friendly, and full of life. I have no doubt that his and Grandma's spirit were present that night, enjoying the same music and festivities that I enjoyed. It is also interesting that Gramp noted the *drive from Balleyvaughn to Doolin, considering we took that very drive this weekend. It is a beautiful drive through the Burren and along Galway Bay, and I know Gram and Gramp, as avid travelers, must have enjoyed the scenery very much.*

It is hard not to feel the presence of my ancestors in Ireland. The people are so much like me, and I am realizing that it is because we share a very common history. Today, in my medieval Irish history class, the teacher was talking about "our" ancestors, as in the ancestors of the Irish students. I realized, however, that the medieval history is actually my history too, just as much as it is the history of the Irish students. I suppose this is insignificant, but it is still a connection with my ancestry that I feel over here.

Bill's travels in Ireland and Peter's lost wallet notwithstanding, my children have not had many thin-place experiences—or, if they have, I haven't heard about them. But they have expressed their reaction to the events surrounding their grandparents' deaths in other ways. Just a few days ago, as I sat down to write a section of this book, the screen displayed an essay, last night's homework that our youngest son, Tim, had written for his high school religion class. His assignment was to share an experience that helped strengthen his faith:

Freshman year, both of my mom's parents died within a couple of months of each other. My grandpa died first of lung cancer, and my grandma died about three months later. This was obviously very hard on all of my extended family. Although just about all of us got to say our good-byes, both of their deaths happened rather quickly. The way my aunts and uncles dealt with it is what has inspired me.

My aunts and uncles, and my mother, got through that entire situation because of their faith. My grandparents were very religious people. When my grandpa was dying, he would say to everyone, "Keep the faith, and the faith will keep you." That was the message he wanted people to get from him. My mom and her siblings really took this to heart during that very difficult stretch of months. They would gather together and talk about how great their parents were, and how everything was in God's plan. They took great comfort in that idea.

The strength that my aunts and uncles, and in particular, my mother, showed when their parents were dying and after their deaths made me look at faith in a new way. I saw that faith can be the most comforting thing for someone during an extremely difficult time. My mom has told me that she doesn't know how anyone could ever go through something like that without a strong faith. How could they take any comfort in the passing of a loved one if they do not believe that there is something to look forward to after life?

I have come to look at faith as something that can have power that is unmatched by anything else in this world. I can't think of anything that could have brought my mother more comfort in the situation she was in than her faith in a greater power. She honestly believes that her parents are with God now, and are happy together.

After this entire experience, I feel like I need to believe in something in my life, especially when I am an adult. I know that I am going to have to go through difficult things in my life, and I want to have the comfort of faith when those things come around.

Reading Tim's essay brought tears to my eyes as I realized the impact my parents' deaths have had not only on me, but on my children and my siblings' children. His essay validated something we all have learned about thin places: that in sharing our stories, we share all of the lessons Mom and Dad taught us about the importance of keeping the faith.

WHERE HOPE DWELLS

"Hope" is the thing with feathers
That perches in the soul
And sings the tunes without the words
And never stops at all.

—EMILY DICKENSON

MAY 1, 2005

A s I write this, it has been three years since my parents died. The thin places connecting our family to Mom and Dad appear less frequently now. But an experience my family and I had during the summer of 2004, a few days before we were to leave on a family vacation to Europe, seemed to sum up many of the thin-place moments I had noticed since their deaths. Appropriately enough, it also involved my *anam cara*, Beth.

Since my parents had loved to travel, and had passed that passion on to their children and grandchildren, Dan and I decided to use some of my small inheritance to take our family on a trip to Europe. Our sons Peter and Bill recently had graduated from college, and we thought this might be our last chance for our family to gather for a two-week vacation before they began their careers. After many discussions about where to go, we decided that a trip to Italy and Switzerland would be perfect. Since Bill was already traveling in Europe with his girlfriend, Dan and I, along with Peter, Emily, and Tim, would hook up with him in Rome.

As a former travel agent, I made all of the airline, hotel, and train reservations. Unfortunately, I missed one not-so-tiny detail that almost derailed our trip. I discovered my oversight just a few days before our scheduled departure, on a day that I had planned to join Beth at the Perpetual Adoration chapel for our weekly hour of prayer. Fifteen minutes before I was to leave for church, I suddenly felt nauseated. I called Beth and left a message saying I felt too sick to leave home. I can't recall an illness coming on so quickly: one minute I felt fine, the next, awful.

Forty-five minutes after calling Beth, as I lay weakly on my family room sofa, a thought popped into my head: *Look at the passports.* Feeling too worn out to obey, I didn't move, mentally arguing, *Dan and I already did that, months ago.* We had both made sure all five passports were safely stored in a drawer in our bedroom. The inner voice, or perhaps it was just a feeling, persisted: *Look again.*

It was now late evening. I dragged myself off the sofa and walked to our bedroom, where Dan was still up and reading. He watched curiously as I removed our five passports from the drawer of our bedside table. As I carefully looked at each one, I gasped: Tim's passport had expired two weeks earlier. I panicked, feeling stupid, discouraged, and helpless all at once, and thinking there was no way we could renew Tim's passport before our departure the following Sunday. I started crying, thinking our family trip of a lifetime was ruined. I silently asked my deceased parents to help: *Dad, Mom— what should we do?*

Within moments, Dan and I started to brainstorm about how to solve this major-league mistake. Suddenly, another thought popped into my head: *Call the airlines.* A sympathetic and helpful agent told me how to check on the Internet for passport offices. Fortunately, the U.S. government has planned for last-minute emergencies and for people like me. It's actually possible to get a passport in one day.

However, you have to go in person to one of the regional passport offices. So, despite the midnight hour, I called the Chicago passport office and used their automated system to make an appointment for three o'clock the next afternoon.

Our son Peter was booked to fly to Europe out of Chicago, where he had just graduated from college. He was spending a few days with us in St. Paul before returning there to catch his flight. Fortunately, he had delayed his return to Chicago by a day. This was a tremendous gift, because he could now help me drive to Chicago with Tim. We had to make the sixteen-hour roundtrip in a day because Tim's last day of school, including final exams, was the day after next.

After a short nap, I woke Peter and Tim at 4:30 A.M. and hit the road. As we approached O'Hare Airport, several miles outside Chicago, Peter had the brilliant idea to leave our car at a park-and-ride lot and take the train into downtown. This meant I could rest rather than worry about Chicago traffic, especially during the rush hour when we left the city later that afternoon. After a quick breakfast at a nearby restaurant, the three of us hopped on the train and arrived downtown shortly after noon.

Peter took Tim to a photo store across the street from the passport office. Meanwhile, I tried to see if we could move up our appointment time since we had arrived early. We filled out the passport application by 1:00 P.M., and were told to return at 3:00 to pick up the actual passport.

I was already tired from the long drive, especially after only two hours of sleep, so we took a cab to Peter's apartment where I could rest for an hour or so. Exhausted, I closed my eyes as soon as we gave directions to the cab driver. I didn't sleep, but kept my eyes closed while Tim and Peter chatted. After fifteen minutes, I sat up straight, opened my eyes, and glanced to my right to see where we were. A half block away, the brick wall of a bar was decorated with shamrocks surrounding the name of the place.

"Boys, look!" I exclaimed. "The name of the bar is the name of the town my father loved in Ireland—Doolin's!" Tim and Peter glanced at each other with raised eyebrows, as if to say, "Here she goes again with another one of her signs."

"Come on, boys—don't you think it's just a little bit interesting that of all the streets in Chicago, we just happened to be traveling down one that has a bar named Doolin's on it? And why did I open my eyes at the exact moment that we passed by it?"

"Mom, it's just a coincidence."

"There's no such thing as coincidences. Not this time, anyway." Silence. "Besides," I continued, "during the height of my hysteria last night, I asked your grandparents to help solve this particular dilemma. Who knows? Maybe *they* reminded me to look at the passports again." After I mentioned my parents, the boys gave up arguing with me.

Later, back at the passport office, I was reassured that I wasn't the only person in America who is oblivious to things like expiration dates on passports. Waiting in a room with fifty or so other folks who had traveled here from all over the Midwest, I chatted with a young man next to me. "What's your story?" I asked, after answering the same question he had already asked me.

"I have a job because of people like you," he said, compassionately leaving the adjective "stupid" out of his remarks. "I work for a courier service that obtains passports for people who need them in one day. Don't feel bad. I'm down in this office every day, so obviously you aren't the only person who goofs up." I smiled, grateful for his kind remarks.

Peter remained in Chicago, while Tim and I returned to our car at the park-and-ride. Once we got beyond the airport, the traffic had eased, so Tim drove for a while. I tried to rest, knowing I would have to stay alert until nearly one o'clock in the morning. To energize myself, I called Dan and Beth on the cell phone when I became tired.

Beth giggled when I told her about the events in the past twenty-four hours. She asked if I could remember what time it was when I looked at the passports. "It must have been sometime just before midnight," I replied. "Why?"

"Well, I did get your message about not feeling well enough to come to Perpetual Adoration. So while I was at the chapel, I prayed for you." Only then did I realize that Beth would have been praying for me at or around the same time that the inner voice told me to look at the passports. I like to think her prayers went to God, who then whispered the message to me.

I admit I don't know how any of this works. Like my children, I've wondered why God would care about my trivial problems, such as disrupted family vacations. I've wondered why I've been so lucky to have so many blessings, including my thin-place experiences. I am no more special than anyone else. But then I remember that, like everyone else, there have been times when God didn't rescue me (or so I thought) from pain and suffering. And there have been times when God didn't answer me (or so I thought) in the midst of a tragic event.

Those doubts, while still present, are less frequent now. Noticing the thin-place events in my life, and hearing about those thin-place events in other lives, has deepened my relationship with God. I now understand that my father's advice, "Keep the faith and the faith will keep you," is so much more than the simplistic platitude I once thought it was. And as I've become more aware of the many ways in which God is present in our lives, it's been easier to keep the faith, to trust in divine providence. And it seems like the more I trust—even when I have no idea where that trust will lead—the greater my reward and the greater my faith.

The world has become, for me, a thin place. By paying attention to how life speaks to me—through the inner voices and messages that do not seem to come from me, and the coincidences that are too serendipitous to have "just happened"—I have discovered greater purpose and meaning in life. A simple formula reminds me how thin places can help us live more fully by discovering and following God's plan for us:

Pay attention to the thin places in our lives.

Reflect on what they mean.

Ask for help from God and others.

Yes! Say this to opportunities and activities that enable us to be channels of God's love and mercy to others.

I have also realized that one of the greatest gifts thin places have given to me has been my soul friendships with my husband, my siblings, and my dearest friends. Beth and others like her have been conduits of God's wisdom, love, and grace, enhancing my own spirituality in so many ways. It was no accident that Beth encouraged me to become a hospice volunteer, a decision that led to a midlife career move that has changed my life. In working with me to discern the presence and meaning of thin places, she helps me discover God's presence in both the best and worst times in my life. In reminding me to "trust that all will be well," she helps me to believe that all *is* well, and that the words of scripture really are true:

> *Again I say to you, if two of you agree on earth about*
> *anything you ask, it will be done for them by my Father*
> *in heaven. For where two or three are gathered in my*
> *name, there am I in the midst of them."*
>
> —Matthew 18: 10–20

Two days before Dad died, I asked him to help me write. I didn't know what I was supposed to write, but I felt it was something I must do. He said he would help me, and I made him a promise in return. "If you help me, Dad," I said, "I promise I will share your strong faith with others, even beyond our family." At the time, I had no idea why I said those words to him.

A few weeks before Mom died, shortly before I used part of her speech in my talk at St. Joseph's Church, I woke with a start in the middle of the night. It was around 3:00 A.M., a time I now believe is "Divine Time," at least for me. It felt as if Dad was in the room with me. I didn't see anything, unlike some people who have visions or dreams of deceased loved ones. But I sensed his presence.

Dad, are you here?

At first, there was no response. Then I heard a voice inside my head say, *You must write.*

Was it my father? As if to answer my question, the message was repeated—not in my mind, but in the language of touch. My hand began to move, but not by my intention or energy; it raised itself. My fingers began to form letters of the manual alphabet, spelling the same message I heard in my head: *You must write.* Thirty-five years earlier, I taken a sign-language class, learning only how to finger-spell. The memory of what I learned then helped me understand the message my fingers were now translating.

My fingers spelled a second message, forming the letters faster than I could have remembered them: *I love you.* Then my hand gently touched my right cheek, caressing it from just below my eye down to my chin. Even though it was *my* hand, the gesture itself was filled with such affection that I knew my father's spirit had touched me, his energy powered by love. My eyes filled with tears and I whispered, "I love you too Dad." Just as he had promised his granddaughter Carolyn, Dad seemed to speak with me "from the other side."

The next day, I received a call from an editor friend, offering her reaction to a short story I had submitted for a book she was editing. "This one is a bit too Catholic for this particular publisher," she said, "but I'm calling you instead of sending you a letter because I want to personally encourage you to keep writing!" The woman's remarks reaffirmed the profound experience I'd had the night before. Because Dad had said he would help me "write something," I interpreted last night's thin-place experience as his way of nudging me to write our family's story. Even before Mom died, I had begun writing about Dad's final days, if only to remember what happened and capture the memories of those days for the rest of my family. Now, I could not refuse his request.

With this book's publication, I have kept my promise to my father and shared his and Mom's deep, unwavering faith in a God who was always with them. I have shared my own faith, by witnessing that thin places exist so that we can experience, on an intimate level, God's love for each of us. I have understood, at long last, that my parents didn't keep their Catholic faith for fear of not getting into heaven; they kept their faith to deal with fear and anxiety, and all the other problems they faced in life. I understand that the prayers and rituals of their religion helped them trust in divine providence, even as they faced death itself. Their faith gave them hope and peace.

My own faith has helped me find hope and peace as well. I no longer have fears about my cancer returning. I live a full life, blessed with meaningful work, a loving husband and children, and the dearest of soul friends. I have embraced the more traditional aspects of my parents' beloved Catholicism, just as Dad accepted the newer forms of prayer, relaxation, and stress-reduction techniques I introduced to him. Along with my own spiritual practices, I now include standard

Catholic rituals and prayers like the daily Mass and the rosary in my daily life. My faith has helped me find God.

My siblings and I believe our parents are with God, and speak directly with God, praying for us now just as they did when they were alive. We interpret all the thin-place signs we have received, and continue to receive, as God's way of reassuring us of Mom and Dad's presence in our lives. The soul is eternal, and the connection we feel to our parents is to their souls—the essence of who they were on earth, the part of them that never dies. We believe that their souls are reunited, not only with each other but also to the God who united them in the first place.

I believe that one day I will be reunited with my parents, Gongie, beloved aunts and uncles, and so many other loved ones. I am comforted by the thought, as I am by the memory of Grandpa Peter's "grace of a happy death." I am excited to meet the God I already know—from paying attention and responding to the thin places in my life. I am certain that death is not the end, and that love does last forever. I am keeping the faith, and I know that it will keep me.

BIBLIOGRAPHY AND RESOURCES

John Ackerman. *Listening to God: Spiritual Formation in the Congregation.* Herdon, Virginia: Alban Press, 2001.

Herbert Benson. *Timeless Healing: The Power and Biology of Belief.* New York: Scribner, 1996.

Dietrich Bonhoeffer. *Letters and Papers from Prison.* New York: MacMillan Publishing Company, 1981.

Marcus J. Borg. *The Heart of Christianity: Rediscovering a Life of Faith.* New York: HarperCollins, 2003.

Barbara Ann Brennan. *Hands of Light.* New York: Bantam Books, 1987.

Julie Cameron. *The Artist's Way.* New York: Jeremy P. Tarcher, 1992.

Joanne Dehmar. "Loyola Letter," Spring 2003, newsletter of Loyola, Spiritual Renewal Resource, St. Paul, Minnesota.

Larry Dossey, M.D. *Healing Words.* New York: HarperCollins, 1993.

Larry Dossey, M.D. *Prayer Is Good Medicine*. San Francisco: Harper-Collins, 1996.

Archbishop Harry Flynn. "Father, husband exemplified grace of a happy death." Archbishop's Column, The Catholic Spirit, February 14, 2003.

Janet O. Hagberg. *Real Power, third edition*. Salem, Wisconsin: Sheffield Publishing Company, 2003.

Janet O. Hagberg and Robert Guelich. *The Critical Journey: Stages in the Life of Faith, second edition*. Salem, Wisconsin: Sheffield Publishing Company, 2005.

Thich Nhat Hanh. *The Miracle of Mindfulness*. Boston: Beacon Press, 1999.

Elisabeth Kübler-Ross. *On Death and Dying*. New York: Macmillan Publishing, 1969.

Steven Levine. *Healing into Life and Death*. New York: Doubleday, 1987.

Dale Matthews, M.D. *The Faith Factor: Proof of the Healing Power of Prayer*. New York: Viking Press, 1998.

John O'Donohue. *Anam Cara*. New York: HarperCollins, 1997.

Mark Peters. "Faith," a poem found on cards and other healing gifts available at www.solacecreek.com.

John D. Powers. *Holy and Human*. Mystic, Connecticut: Twenty-third Publications, 1995.

A. J. Russell, ed. *God Calling*. Uhrichsville, Ohio: Barbour Publishing, originally published in 1939.

Edward C. Sellner. *Wisdom of the Celtic Saints*. Notre Dame, Indiana: Ave Maria Press, 1993.

Linda Smith. *Called into Healing: Reclaiming Our Judeo-Christian Legacy of Healing Touch*. Arvada, Colorado: Healing Touch Spiritual Ministry Press, 2000.

"Thin Places," a newsletter published by Westminster Presbyterian Church, Minneapolis. (Quotes by Reverend John Ackerman, Reverend Timothy Hart-Andersen, and Janet O. Hagberg from various issues.)

Jon Kabat-Zinn. *Full Catastrophe Living.* New York: Bantam Doubleday Dell Publishing Group, 1990.

Jon Kabat-Zinn. *Wherever You Go, There You Are: Mindfulness Meditation in Everyday Life.* New York: Hyperion, 1994.

WEBSITES

www.catholicity.com/prayersdevotions/divinemercy

www.centeringprayer.com/methodcp.htm

www.contemplativeoutreach.org

www.etwn.com/therese/novena

www.healingtouch.net

www.hospice.net

www.htspiritualministry.com

ABOUT THE AUTHOR

M ary Treacy O'Keefe is cofounder and executive director of Well Within (www.wellwithin.org), a nonprofit holistic wellness resource center in West St. Paul, Minnesota, that provides integrative-healing services to people living with chronic and/or life-threatening illnesses. She is a certified spiritual director with a master's degree in theology, and conducts workshops on spirituality and healing. Her writings have appeared in *Catholic Digest*, *Chicken Soup for the Christian Family Soul*, *Stories for a Woman's Heart*, and *Chicken Soup for the Girlfriend's Soul*. *Thin Places* is her first book.

Mary has four grown children and lives with her husband a few miles from her hometown of St. Paul, MN.

Photo by Beth Gedatus

A NOTE FROM THE AUTHOR

Thank you for your interest in *Thin Places: Where Faith Is Affirmed and Hope Dwells.* Perhaps reading my family's story prompted a memory of one (or more) of your own thin-place experiences. If you would like to share an experience or epiphany moment that seemed "meant to be" in your life, it may be included in an upcoming book. Please send your comments regarding this book and/or stories to:

Mary Treacy O'Keefe
P.O. Box 18492
St. Paul, MN 55118
mary.treacy.okeefe@gmail.com
www.marytreacyokeefe.com.

Some of the proceeds from the sale of *Thin Places* will support integrative-healing services at Well Within, as well as the Bill and Terry Treacy Scholarship Fund at Cretin-Derham Hall High School, St. Paul, MN.